MW00413833

Praise for "Jesus Never Said That!"

"I love the James King version!" And, "I already knew James was on to something powerful in writing this book. This was confirmed when I saw the enthusiastic response to James and this topic at our Unity conference. People want to hear these truths!"

> ~ *Rev. Margaret Hiller, Minister, Unity of Myrtle Beach*

"This book is just what we need: an honest, heartfelt and objective look at Jesus' words. Rev. James originally comes from a traditional background and respectfully shows us a new way of hearing Jesus. His book is not New Thought, or New Age, but really "Old Thought and Old Age". Thank you James!

> ~ *Rev. Ed Kosak, Minister, Unity of Charleston, SC*

"Transformative! This 'James King" interpretation will inform, inspire and change the way you look at many different aspects of religion...From who Jesus was and what he stood for, to his insightful, thought provoking and enlightening views on Heaven, Hell and just about everything in between."

> ~ *Max Bolka, Author of Love Is The Answer...Now, What Was Your Question?*

"Although the founders of "New Thought" metaphysics were centered in the Christ, many today come to New Thought wounded by mainstream theology and are not sure about what to do with Jesus. Rev. James King's revelatory new book reveals Him as completely relevant to our 21st century needs, hopes and dreams. It is a loving re-introduction to the New Testament, and greatly needed."

> ~ *Kell Kearns, Director, Co-producer, "The Consciousness of The Christ: Reclaiming Jesus for a New Humanity*

JESUS NEVER SAID THAT!
But What He Did Say Could Change The World

JESUS NEVER SAID THAT!
But What He Did Say Could Change The World

By James King

Copyright 2015 by James King

Without limiting the rights under copyright reserved above, no part of this publication may be reproduced, stored in or introduced into a retrieval system, or transmitted, in any form, or by any means (electronic, photocopying, recording, or otherwise), without the prior written permission of the copyright owner of this book.

ISBN 13: 978-1515106913
ISBN 10:1515106918

First Edition

CONTENTS

Acknowledgments
Introduction

Acknowledgements

I have so many people to thank for their help and assistance in putting this book together. It is amazing how many talented people came together to make this book happen.

A heartfelt thanks to Max Bolka for his insightful wisdom and feedback; it is a better book because of him.

A sincere thank you to Suzanne Giesemann whose advice was spot on and right when I needed it.

I so appreciate Kel Henry-Herbst for coming in at the last minute with her keen observations and editing skills.

Thanks to Chris Poschmann for proofreading proficiency, and her wonderful comments.

I appreciate all those that read the book and gave me your reviews and thoughts. Thank you James Taylor, Kell Kearns, Cynthia Lukas, Leah Edwards, Susan Torres, Margaret and David Hiller, Ed Kosak, and Dale Worley.

I appreciate our wonderful Unity Community that urged me to write this book.

Thank you to Jan Haire for the back cover picture of Jesus and to Dede Norongolo for my profile picture. Also, a very special thanks to Leah King, who created the cover and got the book ready for print.

Introduction

How can we work with the Bible in its current form and use it for the highest possible good?

Is there a way to look at scripture that is applicable to our lives today?

Are the teachings of Jesus practical?

Do Jesus' teachings reveal positive and workable principles that anyone can use?

What kind of meaning do they have for us now?

For years I read the Bible from a fear-based perspective that I had been taught from an early age. I began reading the Bible as a teenager and would memorize verses and passages with a great desire to learn and grow spiritually. I attended Bible College and learned how to deliver a sermon based on the beliefs and ideas that were mine at the time. It was many years later that I began to question the way in which I had been trained to look at the scriptures.

There came a day when my eyes started to open and I realized that my religious education was lacking something very important. My view of God, at the time pointed to a stern Father figure in the sky that was heavily vested in my obedience. To the point that if I did not obey I would be tossed into an eternal fire at the end of my life. I had always seen Jesus as the kinder part of God that came to appease the wrath of his angry father. I truly admired the "words written in red" that were about Jesus' teachings and it was difficult to reconcile the God of the Old Testament with the loving Shepherd of the New Testament.

After over 30 years of study and research I have concluded that the real message of the Bible is about forgiveness and healing rather than fear and punishment. Jesus did not say and teach the fear based religious values I heard as a young child. When I finally read and studied the Bible from a more objective viewpoint, I was shocked at first to discover what it actually said! I was told as a child that the Bible was the only book that contained all the knowledge there was to know about Divinity. They also said I could only have beliefs that were written down in this one book. I discovered this is a very limited way to look at the Divine Infinite Intelligence by saying, "this is all God ever had to say about anything." The truth is that nature is also a revealing look at how Divinity expresses itself. The Universe we live in reveals many principles about the order and balance of everything in existence. The human body is an amazing piece of biological equipment that holds part of the mystery of life too. In fact everything I can see with my eyes is in some way a look into the divine perspective. Not only this but there are volumes of books and scriptures that point to universal truth that is available to all.

I have thought about writing this book for a long time. At first, I looked around to see if anyone else had already written it and I couldn't find a book anywhere that got to the heart of the issues that everyday people ask me about on a regular basis. The unique contents of this book have to do with answering common questions about what the Bible actually says about God, salvation, heaven, hell and many other ideas that Jesus expressed.

You might say, "Who are you James King to think that you know anything about God or the interpretation of the scripture?" I am like you, a spiritual seeker that had my own unique experiences and has arrived at conclusions that work for me. It is through years of self-study that I have become the person I am today. I have a more positive view of God, myself and the rest of creation. I do not condemn anyone else for their ideas; just don't try to force your beliefs on me without hearing me out.

Every one of us has a right to believe in the God of our understanding and happily be where we are in the moment. I also have that right and this is my way of sharing what I have learned, so far.

There are many fine books about the historical Jesus and what various authors have researched about him. I have read and studied many writings about the different theories about who Jesus was and when he lived. We now know that most of the authors of the New Testament were not the original disciples of Jesus, but were instead those who came later. The canon of the Bible is actually based on remembrances from those who claimed to know the original disciples. There is of course, lots of room for human error along the way. In spite of the difficulty of proving when Jesus lived and who he was, I believe that the principles that have come, no matter how that got here to us, are very powerful and have relevance for our 21st century lives. The living principles of truth never go out of style especially when they work!

My approach is this, I have studied the teachings attributed to Jesus and have found them to be very practical and applicable to my life. I believe in the universal laws that are revealed in these teachings about how I can have a happy and positive life experience. These sayings can make a difference in your life too when you apply the true teachings of Jesus rather than religious assumptions. Cold articles of faith have no sustaining power because they have no life in them. Spirituality is experiential and many beliefs about God are typically based on someone's opinion rather than what Jesus actually taught. The key is to look at these writings in context and see the symbolism that they reveal to us about having a spiritual practice and living at peace in the world. If we see them as sayings and teachings for a better life then we can use them as they were most likely intended. The Bible is a poetic book of stories that are not necessarily meant to be a history book but rather transformational ideas that *point to* the truths of life.

Many different versions and translations of the Bible have been put forth over the years and religious hierarchies often base their beliefs on some form of literal interpretation. Currently there are over 40,000 different Christian denominations in existence with new ones springing up all the time. There is so much confusion about Jesus and what he said that many people have given up on trying to read and understand the Bible. It is perfectly understandable to me why people choose not to believe in a vengeful God with an "anger management" problem.

In writing this book I am simply using the current writings that we have rather than what we think we know about what happened thousands of years ago. I am not saying history doesn't serve a purpose and reveal some important ideas about Jesus and his purpose in the world. *That is just not the point of this book.* Because of religious dogma, many people have a vested interest in what happened in the past. It is amazing how people can project onto what happened two thousand years ago to make it match what they currently believe. "It had to happen the way I believe it did because I couldn't be wrong could I?"

Every chapter will list ideas and phrases that Jesus did not say but has been assigned to him over time. We will then discuss what Jesus actually said based on the various translations we have available today. This book is organized in such a way that it can be read in order of your interest. Each chapter is complete by itself, though you can see the bigger picture by reading it front to back. This book is not against people of any religion, it is a book of ideas for you to ponder for yourself. It does point to the truth that God loves us all and we are all God's Children.

The truth is we don't know what actually happened in the past and much of what we think we know is assumption. I often don't remember what I had for breakfast last week much less what ancient people of the past were up to. The key to life is to be about the business of "what is" and working with what we have available to us now. In this book we will take what we have and use it to serve the highest good for today's world.

I enjoy reading the Bible and imagining what kind of Divine ideas I can glean and use right where I am in my life in the here and now. How can I apply these universal principles to enhance my life and live in these blessings today? I am not waiting for a reward in the afterlife. I am claiming peace, joy, love and prosperity in the trenches of my own experience on a day-by-day basis!

The focus of this book is to uncover the practical beauty and elegance of Jesus' teachings and use them to create heaven on earth right where we need it, here and now. This is one of the reasons I felt compelled to write this book in order to assist others in finding their way back to contentment and peace. I believe it is a worthy mission.

I trust that you will enjoy what I playfully call the "James King Version" and see a thoughtful perspective based on the scriptures we have. Enjoy the book and let me know what you think but do it in love, because love really was the point of all the teachings.

Wouldn't you agree?

Peace,
James

Chapter One

Jesus

Jesus never said: *"I have come to bring you a new religion with newer, stricter rules and even more   binding obligations."*

The teacher rose from his seat and began to read from the prophet Isaiah these words,

"The Spirit of the Lord is on me, because he has anointed me to proclaim good news to the poor. He has sent me to proclaim freedom for the prisoners and recovery of sight for the blind, to set the oppressed free. And He closed the book, gave it back to the attendant and sat down; and the eyes of all in the synagogue were fixed on Him."
~ Luke 4:18-20

Whatever you think of Jesus, he knew how to get attention on behalf of accomplishing his powerful mission. This tall middle-eastern man has been talked about for over two thousand years and there are a multitude of opinions about who he was and what he did.

- *Many see Jesus as the Savior that came to die on the cross for the sins of all humanity.*
- *Others see him as just another prophet with an interesting message.*

- *Some academics will say Jesus did not exist but was actually a myth created and compiled from several different teachers at that time.*

No matter your thoughts about Jesus, his image is embedded deeply within the psyche and mind of billions of people around the world.

But, perhaps Jesus did not come to start a new religion but actually came to teach universal principles, which had the power to heal and transform people's lives. Could it be that Jesus was a spiritual mystic who understood the laws of life and that sharing these ideas was his true mission? Is it possible that Jesus was part of a long line of spiritual teachers who came to show us the liberating power of Divine ideas?

What if we really applied what he said? Is it conceivable that we might actually understand the true purpose of life? Can you imagine people truly living the Jesus ethic in the world today without the trappings of religious dogma? How wonderful it would be if we all chose to live in harmony and treat each other as if we were all kings and queens, and our children princes and princesses of the spiritual kingdom. What if we valued each other to the point where no one was considered an outsider and we only desired to care for each other in the best way possible?

What if heaven could really exist right here on earth?

Jesus said he came to do the will of God. The word *will* in the Aramaic means *God's greatest desire*! I do not think we have scratched the surface yet on how good life could be if we all lived according to the law of loving-kindness. How much love, joy, peace and prosperity can you stand? Can you imagine what God's greatest desire would be for us?

12

God wants happiness, love, abundance and especially an enlightened spirituality that works for all. What would our world look like where everyone was absolutely in love with each other, simply for the sake of love itself?

Humanity's biggest challenge is fear coupled with spiritual immaturity. The fear of loss is behind all of the greed and scarcity that appears in the world. By holding on to what we have with a fearful grip we become prisoners to our own materialistic possessions. There is nothing inherently wrong with having material things. The problem is when we allow things to be more important than people. We are living at a time when there is an authentic spiritual awakening taking place and we have an opportunity to direct our amazing talents and abilities to end much of the world's suffering and pain. With a new focus and a spiritually centered mission we could even bring about the end of war and strife. We are beginning to see wholesale change as people are starting to see their true place and purpose in the world. You won't see it if you are glued to the 24 hour "Constant Negative News" stations. You will see the signs and feel the hunger for change if you choose to have real conversations with the people around you.

What if Jesus stepped into today's world? Have we changed all that much from his time? Would he be disappointed by how we have used his teachings to create more separation and division? Amazingly, the collective ego of humanity is not offering anything new to the world. The Preacher of Ecclesiastes says,

"What has been will be again, what has been done will be done again; there is nothing new under the sun."
~Ecclesiastics 1:9

King Solomon was able to see the continual heartache of living in the same energy and doing business as usual. We are seeing the same cycles of unconsciousness happening over and over again, just as it was then. Until we stop the merry-go-round of repetitious patterns it could go on indefinitely. Jesus did speak of the end-times cycle that can lead to new beginnings. *Now* is the time to create something new and fresh. The end time cycle is really the point where we get off the merry-go-round and do something different.

There is evidence to suggest that the world has gone through many cycles for hundreds of thousands of years and even longer. Some people are in their own end time cycles and others have already begun living in a new era. It is up to each individual to let go of his or her old paradigm and embrace the new. In the end-time cycle there is always something that falls away to make room for something fresh. In the past, humanity's negative ego self-destructs and a seed would arise from the ashes to begin again. We have traversed this cycle of destruction long enough, and the time for transformation is here and now.

Are you ready to become a follower of peaceful ways and enlightened living, thinking, and action? It is time to rethink the message of Jesus the Christ and uncover the simple, yet elegant, teachings he gave us. In the past, his teachings have been interpreted from a legalistic world-view, but I believe the true mission of Jesus was about serving the greatest benefit for all. If you are willing to see the scriptures from a higher-good perspective, then you will definitely gain some wisdom and understanding from the scriptures. We can stop the patterns of the negative-ego and chart a new course toward enlightenment and real freedom.

The time has come for a new revelation about a spirituality that works for all. Are you ready to uncover your true self and live in harmony with the rest of creation?

"Everyone will sit under their own vine and under their own fig tree, and no one will make them afraid, for the Lord has made this promise." ~ Micah 4:4

Let us begin now to view the words of Jesus and all of the scriptures with fresh eyes and a beginners mind.

"Ask and it will be given. Seek and you will find. Knock and the door will be opened for you" ~ Luke 11:9

Now is the time for new beginnings and today is the perfect day to start. If not now, then when and if not you, then who?

Chapter Two

God

Jesus Never Said: *"I am so sorry humans but you will never know God as I do."*

'Hear, O Israel: The Lord our God, the Lord is one."
~Mark 12:29

Many people were taught the Christian fundamentalist concept that told of God as a super human in the sky. God could get quite angry and judgmental but also loved you if you accepted "his" concepts of sin, salvation, heaven and hell. Over the years, however, you may have started to question these ideas and arrive at different conclusions. Today, your feelings and beliefs may be more open-ended and will, therefore, be constantly evolving.

The name God is a label created by human beings to describe the spiritual essence of all life. God is the one universal presence that upholds, supports and nourishes everything. This loving presence dwells within everyone and everything. Holy Spirit, Divine Mind, Infinite Intelligence, Father Mother God are just a few names we use to speak about this universal power. We must redefine how we view God as we continue to grow. It's not that God ever really changes, but our awareness and understanding must change, or we may need to ask ourselves if we are really growing?

There are different acronyms I like to us for G.O.D., such as Grand Operational Design or Ground of Divinity. We can further define God as the playful and creative potential within every human being. There are many positive, practical lessons in the parables of Jesus that can work for you when you apply them. I believe that other religions actually refer to the same one God that Christianity supposes and we can learn much from the study of Taoism, Buddhism and Hinduism as well as many other spiritual practices. Those who have spent time looking at different belief systems have found this research to be helpful and instructive. It's important to have a well-rounded understanding of the world's major religions because God speaks to every culture in a way that is for their greatest benefit.

Most of the major religions contain the ideas of love and service. In fact, there are many similarities that tell us that Divinity is working in and through many of them

Almost everyone has a different image in mind when they refer to God and each religion has their unique take on what divinity is to them. God is big enough to be a part of all religions. We are all children of God with innate divine potential. Religion is actually the search for answers to life's big questions. Could it be that anyone that approaches spirituality with an open heart and mind connects with the same One Source? What if we loosened our definitions about what God is and allowed ourselves to expand our ideas to become more inclusive? Would that better represent what all the spiritual teachers were trying to tell us?

If you want to travel to Chicago Illinois you must start where you are using either the faster Interstate systems or you could travel the scenic route along some back roads. Others may want to fly! The idea is that there are many ways to get there. The same is true with the spiritual path. There is only One God but many ways to make your spiritual connection.

Who are we to think that only our beliefs about God are correct and all the other religions are wrong? That is a very small minded view that holds many people in bondage to ideas they were taught as children and never thought to challenge them.

A Spirit Of Inclusion

Jesus was a spiritual teacher and he preached the ideas of acceptance and inclusiveness. He spoke about universal principles, which assist everyone in discovering his or her inner relationship with divinity. Jesus also had very specific thoughts on how to deal with people who were in conflict with each other. The way in which we interact with each other reflects our beliefs and whether or not we are maturing in our relationship to divinity and accurately representing the truth of what we believe.

"You have heard that it has been said, you shall love your neighbor, and hate your enemy.
But I say unto you, *Love your enemies, bless them that curse you, do good to them that hate you and pray for them which despitefully use you, and persecute you; That you may be the children of your Father, which is in heaven: for he makes his sun to rise on the evil and on the good, and sends rain on the just and on the unjust.*

For if you love them, which love you, what reward have you? Do not even the publicans (non-spiritual) do the same? ~Matthew 5:43 -46

The above words of Jesus are about a new paradigm of living, and reveal an excellent way to live *in love* with everybody. The old way of treating people as enemies is not working. Put your energy into learning how to love, how to bless, how to pray for, and do good deeds for your neighbors. This is true divine activity.

The natural world is a reflection of Divine Intelligence and because a tornado hits one area does not mean that the judgment of God is upon the people. The words above say, "It rains on the just and the unjust." Jesus is simply saying that weather happens as it does, and then provides us with the opportunity to assist each other when we need it.

Perhaps that is the point?

It's easy to love and support people who are reciprocating that love back to us. Divine love goes further, considering everyone as worthy, and is willing to go the extra mile. Whenever a disaster happens it's amazing how kind, generous and even heroic our neighbors can be. This is usually when people are expressing their best nature. Wouldn't it be great if we learned to practice our generosity all the time? There is an amazing Intelligence available to all. Everything you need and want can be found by connecting with this Higher Power. When we act as if we all matter, then we are acting from our true divine nature. A God that is big enough to love everyone without playing favorites is a God I can believe in. How about you?

Quantum Oneness

"Quantum theory thus reveals a basic oneness of the universe." ~*Fritjof Capra*

"On that day you will realize that I am in my Father, and you are in me, and I am in you." ~ *John 14:20*

Quantum theory is the theoretical basis of modern physics that explains the nature and behavior of matter and energy on the atomic and subatomic level and corresponds with what Jesus said about God and humans. God is in us and we are all connected as one. Everything in the universe is made of small sub-atomic particles. These particles are the essence of life also known as the substance of God. The power to create is in every molecule of living matter and is the intelligence that knows how to grow arms and legs. This intelligence has also created millions of worlds and solar systems. The power and potential of creation is inside everything in existence.

Human beings have this same intelligence living in them. If we didn't we wouldn't be here. You do not cause the functioning of your heart, lungs, kidneys or any other organ or system in your body. You don't have to because you are one with God and God is the very activity of your body. Divinity is closer than your breath, and yet big enough to fill the entire universe. Science tells us that our atoms move so fast it gives the appearance that objects are solid. We understand that our bodies are not really solid and if the atoms stopped moving there would barely be enough matter to put on the head of a pin. (Unfortunately, we would still weigh the same amount!). We are spiritual beings kept alive by an invisible power we call God.

"Do you not believe that I am in the Father, and the Father is in me? The words that I say to you I do not speak on my own initiative, but the Father abiding in me does his works. Believe me that I am in the Father and the Father is in me; otherwise believe because of the works themselves." ~ John 14:10-11

Jesus is discussing his intimate connection with divinity. He is relaying the beautiful expression of how the larger Intelligence is living in him and speaking through him. He is literally channeling his own divine nature. We know when The Inner Presence is speaking through us, when we are participating in a sacred union with Spirit, which is our natural state. Jesus was teaching by example about how to work in harmony with this Divine Spirit within. Because of the lack of worthiness taught by many religions, many people find it difficult to feel deserving of this enlightened state, but, it is our birthright, and we all have the capacity to express this divinity! It's the only way to evolve to the next level of consciousness in the world.

Intimacy With Divinity

Peter, James, John and Mary felt this divine intimacy and began to share it the same way Jesus did. By constantly hearing Jesus' teachings and being with him, they were able to feel and connect with their own sense of unity, or oneness consciousness.

"When the Day of Pentecost had fully come, they were all with one accord in one place. And suddenly there came a sound from heaven, as of a rushing mighty wind, and it filled the whole house where they were sitting. Then there appeared to them divided tongues, as of fire, and one sat upon each of them. And they were all filled with the Holy

Spirit and began to speak with other tongues, as the Spirit gave them utterance." ~ Acts 2:2-4

The Day of Pentecost was a celebration in Jewish tradition of the giving of the Torah. So when the Disciples gathered together on the Day of Pentecost in the spirit of oneness they received their own guidance for the mission they were called too. The Master Teacher had promised his disciples they would be empowered to do their work. This empowerment was a realization of the spirit of Truth within them. The scripture quoted above is very poetic and it shows us where God is, and how we can all connect on an inner level for ourselves.

How I interpret this verse for us today is in this way. As we align our hearts and mind with Divinity and wait for direction we will have the experience that will empower us with our purpose and mission. God is breathing us now and as we quiet our minds and listen for guidance we will make a deeper connection with the spiritual Presence that can get the job done. The "speaking with other tongues" is a real experience that some people have but symbolically when the Sacred Spirit is energized within us we soon discover our passionate fire and can speak a "new language" of empowerment and oneness. We are literally filled with a passionate zeal that enables us to fulfill our calling in the world. This seems to happen to people when they are ready to inhabit their true divine nature. Emerson said, "Without enthusiasm nothing is ever accomplished." We must become passionate about everything, including our passion.

If you really want unity consciousness with God with all of your heart then you will not be denied and the empowerment will be drawn to you. You must want it and truly desire it in order to be infused with this spiritual energy. There is also a certain amount of waiting in anticipation for it to arise inside of you. That does not mean you are not active. On the contrary, you are opening up and discovering more than ever before about who and what you are.

God is more than words on a page. Spirit is beyond our words to describe, and that is why poetic language can say so much more by painting a picture for us about the nature of divinity. Our understanding of divinity grows every single day as we seek for understanding. Some people believe it happens all at once through a one time religious experience and then all you have to do is maintain the status quo. This does not allow for spiritual growth and understanding. The revelation of God unfolds a little at a time throughout our lifetime, if we are paying attention.

Secret Identity

Just as Clark Kent was really Superman in disguise, you too are a powerhouse who does not realize your own power. Most people do not know who they are in the truest sense. Yes we are human beings, but we are also more than that. This revelation is what the whole journey of life is truly about. Like Superman you are not originally from earth. You came from a spiritual dimension through your Mother's womb carrying a special mission to share with the planet. You are here to rediscover your Divinity and to express God in your own unique and practical way.

The 12 Disciples became the 12 Apostles with a special mission because they got in touch with their true nature and identity. Once you realize that you too are a super being with extraordinary potential the secret is out and you start to live in the Truth of who you are!

Nature

In the beginning was the Word, and the Word was with God, and the Word was God. He was with God in the beginning. Through him all things were made; without him nothing was made that has been made. In him was

life, and that life was the light of all mankind (creation).
John 1:1-4

One of my favorite activities is to sit near a tree and watch the play of the natural world around me. Through careful observation, we can notice the beautiful expression of divinity in the plants and animals. The Divine Intelligence inhabits the physical world we live in – all of it. It's easy to miss the significance of this if we are full of our own thoughts and ideas about what nature is. We have given names and labels to all that we see, but that doesn't mean we know what it is.

The physical world is an experiential place.

Everything in nature is Love or God expressing itself in physical form. The natural element of water is soothing and refreshing to the body, and the mind. The sunshine on your face is a gift of grace to be savored and enjoyed. Oxygen is all around us embracing our bodies and filling us up - that's love too. The trees are giving and receiving energy with us through a symbiotic relationship. We need the trees and they need us to create life together. We are intimately connected with everyone and everything by walking in this earth paradise. As I walk on the ground, negative ions are feeding my body and restoring healthy cells and molecules. Life is doing its work of giving and receiving.

We don't really walk around on top of the earth; we are in the earth and a part of the natural world. My feet touch the same earth as my brothers and sisters in far off countries do. We are connected together by a living energy field we happen to call God. Human beings are the divine children of this Universal Spirit, as are the plants and animals. Animals freely roam about having no thought of boundaries. They operate as if there is no separation and that's because there isn't. We, as humans, created fences and walls out of fear to keep out what we could not control. All the lines drawn on a map are artificial constructs. We need to remember that separation is an illusion. We are all a part of the same, that one thing, that one energy, that oneness that we call God. We belong with each other or else we wouldn't be here.

Divine Love is what binds us together.

Once you see how the natural world is connected and that God is in everything and everyone you will never see the world in the same way again.

Chapter Three

Hell

Jesus never said: *"God loves you, but if you don't repent, you're going to hell."*

"What is hell? I maintain that it is the suffering of being unable to love." ~Fyodor Dostoyevsky

"The mind is a universe and can make a heaven of hell, a hell of heaven." ~ John Milton

For many years, hell was viewed solely as a place of torment where sinners and wicked people would be relegated at the end of their lives. This view has been ingrained in so many people for so long it can be difficult for us to see it any other way. However, something inside my spirit kept urging me to take a new and fresh look at the scriptures from a different perspective. I looked up all the verses that spoke about the concept of hell and decided I would let the chips fall where they may. Instead of looking at them with a preconceived mind, I simply looked up the words in their original Hebrew and Greek and took them at face value.

Guess what I discovered? The mind can be programed to think a certain way and it's hard to change the old programming.

That's why politics has become such a mess today, because each person is seeing from his or her own biased vantage point. People cannot simply allow the other side to have their own views unless they can tear them down. People sometimes can literally hate the candidate on the other side because of all the propaganda that has been said about them.

Similarly, if someone loves a certain football team, it is rare that they can actually complement the other team for a well-played game when their own team loses. Instead, people will blame the referees or even some superstitious belief about having changed their lucky underwear before the big game.

It's time to move beyond superstitious beliefs that keep us bound to old paradigms, which serve no real positive purpose. We must seek the truth if we want to know the true nature of God and of human beings.

Are you ready to take a look at the Hebrew and Greek words for hell? If you take a look, with an open heart, you will find there are basically three words for hell in the Bible.

Each word has a different meaning. Historically, translators have chosen to interpret all three words as hell. Below are the three words from the Hebrew and the Greek.

- *Sheol (Hebrew) "A grave or pit"*
- *Hades (Greek) "An invisible or unseen place"*
- *Gehenna (Greek) "A trash dump"*

Notice there is no mention of a tailor-made dungeon of torture where souls are being eternally abused in perpetual flames of fire in the afterlife. I don't know about you, but for me this is very good news! If you have been taught the negative view of hell it would seem that I am just making this up, but I am not. These are what the words mean, and I am glad they do, aren't you?

Sheol is the only word in the Old Testament for hell or "the grave". Obviously, in those days when a person died, they were put in a pit or a grave. Today many are opting for cremation, which is simply how we currently handle the physical body after someone dies. In those days the body was buried in the ground out of sight so the bodies could decay back to the earth. Most importantly, this is not the eternal hell taught by some religions.

Hades is one of the words used in the New Testament for hell and is an *unseen place*. The word was borrowed from Greek mythology and had nothing to do with eternal torture in the afterlife. If you and a friend were hiding out, you could be said to be in *hades* or a *hidden area* where no one could see you. But nowhere is it a hell of everlasting torture and punishment that some preachers seem to relish in talking about.

Gehenna is the other word used in the New Testament for hell and does involve fire, but not in the afterlife. Gehenna was the garbage dump outside the city where refuse was burned. There was a continual fire burning so they could get rid of their trash. The haul away system we enjoy today did not exist. The words hell fire in the Bible was often translated as Gehenna, which was derived from an actual valley near Jerusalem. The valley (or dump) of Hinnom is where refuse and dead bodies were placed to be burned up.

When Jesus used these words he was speaking metaphorically just as was his way of teaching. He compared the burning anguish of a Soul who feels separate from God to the fires of Gehenna or the trash dump. We still use this metaphor today. When we are depressed, we say we are "down in the dumps". So, where is the Hell that so many preachers have spoken about? It's certainly not in the Bible!

Some scholars believe the concept of hell fire became popularized when the book "Dante's Inferno" began to be widely read in the late 1400's, after the printing press was invented. This is a book written from Dante's imagination, a man who created different levels of suffering and hellish torment for his story. As you can see, the definitions of these words from the Bible do not support a torture chamber of endless suffering for lost souls. Jesus NEVER taught this idea and it is an insult to Divinity and authentic spiritual seekers to believe in such a fear-based doctrine!

Can we let this go now?

If the official doctrine of hell was so important to Jesus (as it is to some religious leaders), then why didn't Jesus explicitly say that one must accept him as one's "personal savior" to get to "heaven?"

We cannot take everything written in the Bible as absolute, literal truth. There are other, violent and nonsensical "dogmas" which some writers of the Bible advance. For example, Paul tells us in Ephesians 6:5 that slavery is part of the natural order. But modern society has rejected and outgrown this idea.

If we blindly accepted all of these ideas, we would return to a medieval state of existence. For example: How about stoning a woman to death because her husband suspects she has committed adultery? In today's world we don't

29

believe that people commit adultery by marrying a divorced person.

The consciousness of people in ancient times was at a very low level of understanding and was almost exclusively about survival. They were very fearful for their lives and did not live very long. At the same time they still had a capacity to understand truth at the level they could receive it. The Bible is a great book to gain wisdom and inspiration from, but it has to be interpreted from a non-literal standpoint or it won't make sense. Or just from a historical or cultural view point too. These "rules" that were put into a place were to help the people at the time survive and reproduce... Seafood and pork were "bad" because they ate garbage, which could have made people sick.

To believe that the loving Presence of God would forever leave millions of lost souls in a last day fire-pit is the ultimate abandonment. This belief has created deep-seated anger and guilt in lots of people. It's so important that people are healed from this horrible doctrine that Jesus never actually taught.

Once you experience the unconditional love representative of the true Divine nature, you will grow and change without the grim fear of punishment. It's time to silence your inner terrorist and allow a great peace to come to you. The irrational fear of a punishing God is a worn out concept that needs to be released from our consciousness. God will never abandon his creation because it's all made from the very essence of Divinity. It would be like God abandoning him or herself. We are all God's children and we are loved unconditionally. If we, as humans, still love our offspring no matter what... even if they do something that we don't approve of... then how can we say that God would do that to us?

Letting go of a fear-based idea is difficult for people who have heard it over and over as children. It gets rooted inside the emotional body and affects people at a deep level.

You will find comfort and real inner peace knowing there are other ways to look at the Bible, which reflect a divine loving kindness.

God is good, everyone is sacred and nobody will go to a fiery place of suffering in the afterlife...

Jesus never said that!

Chapter Four

Heaven

Jesus never said: Claim your mansion in the sky!

"Heaven is under our feet as well as over our heads."
~ Henry David Thoreau

"The dog is a gentleman; I hope to go to his heaven not man's." ~ Mark Twain

Just as there are many misconceptions about Hell, there are lots of teachings about heaven that are not found in the Bible at all, or are taken way out of context. Many of these thoughts and ideas came about within the last few hundred years. Preachers chose to hold the carrot instead of using the stick, and were constantly emphasizing the glories of going to heaven in order to get people to buy into their teachings. They promised mansions, streets of gold, crowns, pearly gates and white robes. Many hymnbooks are filled with these kinds of sentiments. The problem with this is that it turns the gospel into a materialistic religion whose adherents are looking for the proverbial, "lifestyles of the rich and famous," in the afterlife.

"In my Father's house are many 'Mansions' (rooms)."
~ John 14:2

Why would you need a mansion in the afterlife? Especially since you will be a spirit and you won't need a kitchen most likely because a spirit does not have to eat physical food. You also wouldn't need a bedroom because spirits do not need to sleep. Bathrooms are unnecessary too and living rooms with couches and chairs are not needed either. Cable TV in heaven, I don't think so. Do spirits just hang out and haunt mansions that they can't make use of?

The word *mansion* is only mentioned in the King James Bible and is really the idea of an *inner room*; a *state of being that exists within divinity*. It is the idea of dwelling in an inner state of grace and joy.

In the world we can quickly grow tired of external dwellings and material objects, but the spirit within contains the real "heaven". The Mind of God is our true home and is total bliss when we abide there in a consistent way. Our true abode is divine consciousness and oneness with divinity. The "Pearly Gates" idea is a quote taken from the Book of Revelation and does not refer to a literal set of gates in the afterlife.

> *"And the twelve gates were twelve pearls; each one of the gates was a single pearl. And the street of the city was pure gold, like transparent glass." ~ Revelation 21:21*

The above verse reveals a symbolic vision about how the city of Jerusalem was compared to a spiritual idea. The Book of Revelation is not about the end of the world or a bloody Armageddon scenario. It is one man's visions and dreams about his relationship with divinity.

If there ever was a metaphorical book then the Book of Revelation is a prime example! Seven headed dragons, seven candlesticks and the four horsemen of the apocalypse. There are beasts rising out of the sea, and other fantastic pictures that can only be considered *symbolism for spiritual ideas.* You cannot interpret this book literally. You can try, but it would be like saying the story of "Alice in Wonderland" was based on a true and factual story. Rather, it is a visionary experience much like a dream. The book of Revelation is very symbolic and does contain many beautiful metaphysical truths in its pages. Let's look at just some of the spiritual riches found in it.

When the street of gold is mentioned in the Book of Revelation it represents a person who has fully developed and realized his or her divine potential. This "one gold street" is symbolic of the spiritual oneness we can all experience when we connect with our own state of natural divinity. Gold is rare and precious and makes a good symbol for divinity. The gold we are to seek lies within our own beings. The idea here is to realize our own value and preciousness and thus see that we all have a golden nature. We are divine beings with the potential to express the highest forms of love and compassion and become a gold street or path for others to follow. One who loves totally and completely is pure gold.

All the symbolic numbers mentioned in Revelation represent various ideas of truth and wisdom. For example the number 12 is a number of divine beauty and overcoming. 7 is the number of perfection and completion. 144,000 virgins represent a group of overcoming individuals that have reclaimed their true nature. But it is not a literal number! It would be such a limitation to think that only 144,000 people would experience union with God. The idea of being a virgin in this context is not about sexual relations but about spiritual purity.

The first verse in the Book of *Revelation* reveals some clues about the spiritual truths of this manuscript.

*"**The Revelation of Jesus Christ**, which God gave Him to show to His bond-servants, the things which must **soon take place;** and He sent and communicated it by His angel to His bond-servant John." ~ Revelation 1:1*

It is the Revelation of Jesus Christ that Spirit gave to John! It does not say Revelations in the plural sense. This is an inner revelation of the Christ within you. These things must *soon take place* and not to be a literal *end of the world* scenario happening in our current day. Prophecy teachers pull all kinds of strange ideas from this book. Many of them have turned the *end of the world* prophecy teaching into big business. Fear has been a big driver of these kinds of books and products for a long time but now we are ready to let go of these childish fears. There are even Ministers currently selling bulk powdered food supplies and generators to prepare folks for the end times. Of course, if you are the only person on the block with food guess where everybody is going for dinner?

Like the rest of the Bible, The Book of Revelation is a metaphorical book on how to live an enlightened life right here and right now.

In my early years, I read lots of these fear based books and heard many sermons and teachings about the "end of the world". These teachings did not help me become a better person but they did engender more fear, dread, guilt, confusion, self-loathing and other unnatural feelings that took years for me to work through.

Jesus never said only the "saved" would go to heaven and *Jesus never said* that the "unsaved" would go to hell.

The word "unsaved" is not found in the Bible anywhere so in my understanding there is no such thing as an "unsaved" individual. Jesus did speak in terms of discerning the difference between being righteous and unrighteous, which had a different meaning in the mind of the ancients than people think of it today. *The word righteousness is not about trying to be nice or good. It is about aligning yourself with the Divine.* It means to align with the will and purpose of the mind of God. That may sound difficult or even impossible, but it is not.

Righteousness = Right Mindedness

To be in your right mind is to stay connected with the Mind of God. It is actually about the practice of joining ourselves to a higher state of being. Our little minds cannot see the bigger picture, but the Higher Mind can. When we follow and listen to the Higher Mind we are aligned rightly with truth, love and wisdom.

Therefore righteousness is not as much about our doing as it is our being. If I live in a righteous state then I am continually practicing my connection to divinity. In this way I am in my right mind!

So, What Does Happen When We Die?

Where do we go? Does our soul survive the body? Is there really a heaven where souls will reside after death? Did Jesus ever say that only the "saved and sanctified folks" would go to heaven when they die? Let's see what we can uncover from the Bible about the afterlife.

36

After six days Jesus took with him Peter, James and John the brother of James, and led them up a high mountain by themselves. There he was transfigured before them. His face shone like the sun, and his clothes became as white as the light. ~Matthew 17:1-3

When we die the only thing that happens is our physical body stops functioning, but we as spirit beings continue on. Spirit cannot die, but it changes form. We all have an inner body made of the energy of light that we adapt to when we pass from this world. This inner body is a container of all of the thoughts, feelings and intentions we have ever had. This is the part that survives what is called death. The story of Jesus transfiguration shows us how the inner body of light and energy is what we truly are. Whenever someone ascends a *high mountain* in scripture it means that they are having a spiritual experience of some kind. The three disciples saw Jesus in his true form as energy and light. The reason they were able to see it in Jesus is because they had this same essence within them.

"For from him and through him and to him are all things (beings)." ~ Romans 11:36

We all came *from* God or unconditional love and we will all *return* to unconditional love. Our spirit is made of the substance of God and cannot be destroyed! There is no earthly substance that can kill or destroy the spirit of a person.

The Spirit is indestructible and will never wear out nor is burned up. When Jesus spoke of fire in the scripture he was speaking about passion and zeal. When our spirit is on fire with Spiritual Presence we are living in our true passion and calling. Many churches have built their total belief systems on this idea of escaping hell and entering heaven based upon whether you have your salvation ticket or not. But, **Jesus never said** much about the afterlife.

You won't be able to say, 'Here it is!' or 'It's over there!'
For the Kingdom of God is already within you."
~Luke 17:21

He is telling us to pay no attention to those that say the Kingdom of heaven is a literal place somewhere. The kingdom of heaven is in our midst and within us. So, death is simply moving more fully into that inner heavenly spiritual state of being. The good news is that it is available right now. It is within your reach because it is what you really are.

"Behold I make all things new." ~ *Revelation 21:5*

Heaven and hell are truly states of being. When we practice our connection to divinity we experience the peaceful union that generates joy and all good things. If on the other hand we allow our negative egos to run our lives then we experience a lower quality of life experience. Hell is a state of mind that is full of self-torture, self-blame and false accusation. When the mind is allowed to hang out in the lower frequencies of hellish thought it falls prey to depression and fear. The outward world of effects is not what controls us. The inner state of thought, feelings and emotion create the world we live in right now.

The Spiritual World

The spiritual world is teeming with life of all kinds. Heaven is not *over yonder* in a far off universe millions of miles away. Your loved ones are still with you sending messages of encouragement and keeping in touch. Heaven is all around us filled with angels and spirits of great light

38

that are fulfilling their high purpose of service. There are celestial beings of such unimaginable love that the hardest heart would instantly melt in their presence. Don't believe it? Relax your mind and let yourself drift into a state of wonder and see how you feel. See if you notice the refined and subtle energies that arise when the mind is still. This space is where divine ideas and all kinds of inspiration come from. When we let go of our fixed concepts of how we think the world should be that is when we can experience the real world, as it is.

We co-create with Divinity the afterlife we are to experience. In other words, it will be what we need it to be. If we need healing after a long and challenging life, then Spirit will work with us to renew and restore our energy and bring us back to balance. If we felt isolated and rejected, then Spirit will accept us and love us back to wholeness. Whatever our experience in this life was, we will find grace and peace in the afterlife. Divine Spirit is unconditionally loving and accepting of all - always! Fear must be overcome so that healing and restoration can finally come to all people. Heaven is here with you now and heaven will only lead to more heaven, whether in this life or the next!

It's time to reframe these fear-based ideas about divinity and step into the sunshine of Divine Love.

Chapter Five

Religious Personae

Jesus never said: *"Blessed are the 'chosen' for they shall be called the real children of God."*

"One of the blunders religious people are particularly fond of making is the attempt to be more spiritual than God"
~ Frederick Buechner

"Beware of the yeast of the Pharisees, because they are hypocrites. Everything that is hidden will be shown, and everything that is secret will be made known. What you have said in the dark will be heard in the light, and what you have whispered in an inner room will be shouted from the housetops." ~ Luke 12:1-3

I Am Fair-I-See

A few years ago a well-known evangelist was condemning people for their sexual sins. I heard him deliver a loud and over the top sermon that was very specific about the "wrong-doings" of others with whom he disagreed. A couple of weeks later he was caught in a hotel room with a prostitute. The behavior he preached against was the very activity he was engaged in! When we live without compassion invariably the day comes when we need it and it is not there for us. Hypocrisy is nothing new and has

40

been around since the beginning of time. Everything hidden in the "inner room" of the heart and mind needs to be revealed and brought out into the open. The secret issues have to be shown for what they really are and dealt with. If your core foundation is built on resentment and bitterness there can be no peace until the secret issues of the heart are revealed and healed.

The Pharisees were the religious leaders of Jesus' day. They felt they were already righteous and absolutely knew what God wanted for them and everyone else, too. Unfortunately, it was all a show and there was no real substance to their teaching and because of their superficiality, Jesus called them hypocrites.

True Spirituality Leads To Inner Healing And Wholeness.

The Pharisees only knew how to cover up the hidden issues and then feign religious piety. They wore the mask of a religious persona that is still going on today. The word Pharisee means "the separated ones." On several occasions Jesus quoted the prophets who said, "God desires mercy more than sacrifice." He reserved a special and pointed message for the scribes and Pharisees as we look at some of the words that Jesus actually said. In the Gospel of Matthew, Jesus called them *hypocrites*, a term in the Greek language that applied to actors or people who were pretenders, saying one thing but acting in a different manner.

The Pharisees were very strict in their interpretation of the Jewish laws, which made them feel superior to others. They loved to ridicule and persecute common people with impossible rules and rituals, which had to be performed properly (according to them), or you were considered less

41

than adequate. Their false religious piety was on display for everyone to behold. Jesus said they loved to put on a show with their self-righteous and dramatic prayers on the street corners. It was an act and was not sincere.

"Woe to you, scribes and Pharisees, hypocrites! For you are like to white washed sepulchers, which indeed appear beautiful outward, but are within full of dead men's bones, and of all uncleanness." ~ Matthew 23:27

I can almost hear the Pharisees say "Come one, come all and see how pious we are and see how we have the truth that nobody else has!" Jesus was actually commenting on their lack of spiritual connection with Divinity and on their great concern for how they appeared to others. Unfortunately, the "us four and no more" philosophy is still making the rounds today. People are constantly creating rules within their church to denote the in-group versus the out-group. You are either a part of their special club, or you're not, and if you aren't... you're going to a really bad place when you die.

I Am Sad-You-See

The Sadducees were the Jewish aristocracy who enjoyed the many benefits from hanging out with the upper crust of Roman culture. During Jesus' time they controlled the high Jewish council called the Sanhedrin. They were pompous beyond belief and greatly despised by the common people. Both the Pharisees and the Sadducees were in competition with each other, similar to our modern religious fundamentalists and self-serving politicians in many ways. Their negative egos never seem to stray far from fear, guilt and manipulation.

The "separated ones" still exist today and believe they are not only better than others, but are more right than others, too. Many religious television programs exist today where preachers pronounce judgment on anyone who does not see things his or her way, though there are subtle signs that they are starting to fade out of favor with authentic seekers. Many people today report and share the heavy and negative doctrinal burdens under which they grew up. They are still dealing with the painful aftermath, even into adulthood. Religious guilt tends to stick like molasses and seems to require a lot of hard work to get beyond it. The teachings of Jesus were counter to these religious leaders, and they did not like it one bit. They felt their power over the common person was being challenged and they were not used to that. Similarly, the religious personalities of today do not look kindly upon their ideas being challenged by people "looking in" from the outside. "How dare they challenge me? Don't they know I am doing this for God?"

"When Jesus had finished saying these things, the crowds were amazed at his teaching, for he taught with real authority--quite unlike their teachers of religious law."
~Matthew 7:28-29

A true spiritual teacher has direct knowledge of God and does not need to pretend to be something he or she is not. More than anything else in our modern world, we are hungry for direct individual connection with the Infinite Intelligence. We want to know what all the teachers of wisdom knew, but we need a fresh approach so we can apply it to our lives now. We must let go of religious dogma and political posturing. Jesus taught real spiritual answers and creative solutions to common challenges. He shared simple stories and parables, which bypassed the self-righteous leaders in order to reach the people who had an open heart and a ready mind. The spirit of the

Pharisees and Sadducees still exists today. We need to stop giving our power away to these kinds of leaders simply because they are good actors that know how to put on a good show.

> *"Beware of the scribes, who like to walk around in long robes, and love greetings in the marketplaces and the best seats in the synagogues and the places of honor at feasts, which devour widows' houses and for a pretense make long prayers. They will receive the greater condemnation. " ~ Luke 20:46-47*

Misery really does love company, and religious leaders who use guilt and manipulation already feel condemned within themselves. They are more than willing to share their misery with you, using literal interpretations of the Bible as support material for doing so. Because of the ego's singular focus on the external world people have missed the truth of the indwelling presence of God. Jesus was hard on these religious rulers because they were abusing the true spiritual practice of the heart and turning it into burdensome rules, which had no life in them.

We all have to release our false religious personae, or we may find ourselves operating as the pretenders and hypocrites of which Jesus spoke. Superiority and self-righteousness keep us from looking within and unearthing our wholeness. I must release the Pharisee in me so that the heart can take over and lead me home.

Authentic Spirituality

God has always been with you. You can find peace right now by taking a deep breath and begin your journey to uncover the divinity inside your own being. Once you remove the false personae you have created, you can be free to seek true spiritual freedom and authenticity.

> *"You know that the rulers in this world lord it over their people, and officials flaunt their authority over those under them. But among you it will be different. Whoever wants to be a leader among you must be your servant, and whoever wants to be first among you must be the servant of everyone else. For even the Son of Man came not to be served but to serve others." ~ Mark 10:42-45*

The Divine is the ultimate servant and is the true source underneath all life. The teachings of Jesus lift all people, not just the religious powerbrokers. Service to others is a universal principle that connects us. There can be no *me* without *we*. We need each other more than we sometimes may be willing to admit. If we really want to be like Jesus then sacred service is what we ought to focus on. Authenticity is more than just a spiritual buzzword, and is something that is absolutely needed in the world today. You will discover your place in the world and the beautiful gifts you have to share by acting from your true and authentic self. You are already a child of God, with nothing more to prove. This is the true grace of Jesus' teachings. We must remove the mask of our religious personae and uncover the natural self that we already are. Our collective religious personae create a wall between people. This wall of separation also makes enemies of those who do not agree with us. Jesus understood how religious personae kept people from finding their true core identity. It is the greatest barrier between true connected spirituality and religious bad acting.

One of the biggest challenges we face in the world today is learning how to live from our heart center. Religion without heart can become a bully and can even kill in the

45

name of God. Terrorism is error thinking and results from a literal and negative view of Divinity. When God is seen as the great judge who is keeping score between his faithful and all the "others," all kinds of posturing and confusion arises.

It's interesting to note how many churches keep careful records on the number of converts they make to their special brand of religion, but never keep any record of how many millions they drive away from authentic spirituality with their list of rules and regulations that all but their select few can live up to. Fairness would seem to dictate that both sides of the ledger be maintained. The fact is, many churches turn far more people away from the real teachings of Jesus, and instead torment them with outward rules of dos and don'ts.

Authentic spirituality is what the religious persona *thinks* it has, but authentic spirituality doesn't lead people to hate or condemn themselves. It leads people to accept and love themselves, no matter what. Authentic spirituality is what someone has when they kneel down with a person in pain and help them up, making no judgments about their past, present or future. Authentic spirituality is also what someone has when they lovingly assist a person to become a positive and whole version of themselves, rather than what *they want that person to be!*

Remember, the religious persona is the false sense of self that imitates the true spiritual Self and is the *number one block to true spirituality*. It is the biggest hindrance to the ever-unfolding revelation of Divinity. It also keeps people in a state of fear and guilt. Letting it go is the best gift you can give to yourself.

Many people are convinced God will smite them and cast them into a horrible pit in the afterlife if they don't get the word out about their religion. It is very stressful to live under that kind of threat. Fear of judgment causes people to act out in fearful and anxious ways. If what I do is based on trying to please God out of fear, then I am living under a false and heavy burden. Are you ready to drop your religious persona and live from a place of grace and peace?

Jesus did say:

"Take my yoke upon you. Let me teach you, because I am humble and gentle at heart, and you will find rest for your souls." ~ Matthew 11:29

No worries, just a peaceful connection with Divinity.

Chapter Six

Storyteller

Jesus never said: *"Please take everything I say literally"*

"Jesus spoke all these things to the crowd in parables; <u>he did not say anything to them without using a parable</u>."
~Matthew 13:39

"With many such parables he was speaking the word to them, so far as they were able to hear it; and he did not speak to them without a parable; but he was explaining everything privately to his own disciples."
~ Mark 4:33-34

When Jesus spoke to the masses, his teaching style was to share stories and illustrations to describe a way of life that he often referred to as the kingdom of heaven. He was speaking from a holistic and spiritual perspective. When people were able to see the truth of the stories he shared, it could bring about real change and transformation in their lives. Going through the various scriptures you will see how the teachings of Jesus were based on a very positive psychological and spiritual understanding meant to bring a sense of healing and well being.

Unfortunately, the Bible has been used as a wedge to separate people from each other. You and I don't have to use it in that way. The scriptures came to us over many years from several authors and several different translations. Different theologians have interpreted the Bible from their own particular denominational slant. Therefore, the Bible is looked at through the biased lens of culture and outdated tradition. Today we have a document that still contains Truth in it, just not in a literal sense. We must look at the Bible with fresh eyes, along with a desire to find its true usefulness.

> *"The letter kills but the spirit gives life."*
> *~ II Corinthians 3:6*

If the letter kills or blocks the spirit, then we should not make the literal interpretation the main thrust. The Bible was written from an Eastern point of view, which is different from the Western perspective. The Eastern mind views life from an inner awareness, whereas the Western mind views life from more of an outward perspective. When we try to interpret the Bible from a literal mind set we can miss the whole point of what is being said. By the time you throw in the differences in culture, customs, language and Western interpretation, the teachings may not even be close to what the original writers intended.

Most people of that time could not read or write, so the way they carried forth Jesus' teachings was from an oral tradition. The best way they had to communicate a belief was to share a story. That story would have a point to it and that point was the truth they wanted to convey. Everything Jesus discussed with the masses was spoken in story form as a parable. He would break down and clarify his teaching points with his close disciples because he was training them to carry his message of healing and wellbeing to the world.

Jesus never said anything publicly that was not expressed as a parable, which is an analogy or story. Everything he shared was designed to be a teaching that illustrated universal truths. When we really understand this simple idea we are then able to perceive powerful spiritual truths from his teachings. Jesus taught strictly through metaphors and sayings because, in truth, all of life is a metaphor. To get the message of what life is telling us is to get the point that will lead us to a truly fulfilling spiritual experience. There are no accidents. The Divine has been leading us all along as we learn to recognize it.

Many great teachings have been handed down throughout the ages, and genuine truth is what links them all together. The greatest metaphors of life become a golden thread of truth, revealing to us the symbols about how life works. The stories may or may not have actually happened, but that is not really the point.

A Whale Of A Story

I was in a bookstore one day drinking some tea and leafing through a magazine when I overheard two ladies talking about the Bible. They were discussing the story of Jonah and the whale, a story many of us heard as children in Sunday school. One of the ladies was convinced the story was literally true and the other felt it was not a real whale that swallowed Jonah. They both were insistent and argued the point for quite some time.

In my mind the point was not whether it was literal or not, but that Jonah had allowed himself to be swallowed up by life's circumstances and resisting the flow of his life's path. Jonah was not a happy person. He was suffering because he was fighting against his mission. He was in denial of his destiny and life purpose. Haven't we all gone through difficult circumstances like this at some time or another?

The beauty of a parable or a story is not whether Jonah was literally swallowed by a whale, but the fact that the spiritual lesson of true surrender would make his life (and yours and mine) a lot better! We have always had stories from every culture that we can learn from. Fairy tales are not literally true, but they contain many wonderful revelations about life, and we can learn much from their symbolism. If God or the Divine energy is in all things as it says in John 1:1-4, then all creation, even that of humans through writing or song, is divinely created. We can derive spiritual nourishment through everything, not just certain "approved" books and writings, as some religious leaders would have us believe.

A Kiss Of Awakening

To awaken the sleeping princess with a kiss is a metaphor about awakening the spirit of Divinity within each of us. The kiss represents the need for gentle compassion and loving-kindness to facilitate our awakening. Isn't that what we all need? The wicked stepmother symbolizes the bitter and resentful person who tries to poison us with the rotten apples of shame and guilt.

When we accept teachings based in fear and anger, it can affect and influence us to the degree that we fall into the trance of everyday life because we become to worried and anxious about doing the "wrong" thing that we miss the real spiritual qualities of our true selves. Fear teaches us to get in line and stay there or bad, bad things will happen to us, and this is the story of fear based religion, the kind that so many people have been hurt by. Many sleeping beauties today need the truth of a parable or story to awaken their spirit and see the light of their *inner beauty.*

There are some great allegories, which teach positive life principles, to be found in the Bible. These stories contain wisdom keys to unlock the mental and spiritual prisons we often find ourselves in. A good story can shift our thinking just enough to set us on a new and more expanded path that could not even be considered before. A well-shared story can remove the scales from ones eyes so the truth can more clearly be seen.

"A storyteller makes up things to help other people; a liar makes up things to help himself." ~ Daniel Wallace

When the Bible says Jesus only spoke in parables, it is not taking away anything from the truth he shared. In fact, the Bible becomes even more useful and helpful to us. Allegories are really universal truths applicable to everyone in a practical way. Many of the stories Jesus told may not have been literally true. However, the real truth is not in the facts of what happened, but in the point of the story. I think parables are useful in that they meet us where we are and allow us to get the spiritual nourishment and truth out of them that we need when we need it. They make the truths more relatable in that way.

Can you see the difference?

For example, in the book of Romans it says,

"He is not a Jew which is one outwardly, but he is a Jew which is one inwardly and circumcision is that of the heart, in the spirit, not in the letter." ~ Romans 2:28-29

This puts the whole concept of the journey of the Jewish people in perspective. Every one of us is the chosen people of God, and Spirit works with each of us according to what we need to awaken us. The Jewish people, in this case, represent anyone that has begun their spiritual journey in earnest.

The Jews wandered in the desert for 40 years experiencing every trial imaginable, and making plenty of mistakes. Some of them learned, and of course, many did not. Isn't that the case in modern society? Some are leading by example to create a better life for themselves and the world, while others are still wandering around in the dry deserts of outdated traditions based in fear. We all have a choice to hear the stories and make the changes we need in order to heal ourselves of whatever stands in the way of our spiritual growth.

The parables of Jesus are very practical and liberating when we use them in this positive way.

Western theologians tend to view the Bible literally and more dogmatically. This is contrary to how it was spoken and written because the Eastern culture intends for a multilayered understanding of the wisdom teachings to be conveyed.

Our Western world likes to use words to hold people to the letter of what is being said. Even the media tends to be like lawyers endeavoring to trip up politicians and catch them in a misspoken word. Of course the politicians are very good at parsing their own words so they cannot be labeled and put into a certain box. One famous politician demonstrated this point in his answer to a specific question, when he said, "It depends on what your definition of 'is' is."

That is how far off we are from Jesus the storyteller and his sharing symbols of truth, which give spiritual guidance to the hearer, rather than binding them to certain religious rules. Trying to live according to the letter of the law denies the grace of a simple story that helps a person learn a valuable truth. A story may contain several eye-opening ideas, which can help a person to grow spiritually. Spiritual growth is the bottom line of all the teachings that Jesus gave. It is time to re-evaluate our beliefs and prove what really works and what has life in it.

"Little children, let us not love in word or talk but in deed and in truth." ~ 1 John 3:1

Chapter Seven

Metaphysical Truth

Jesus never said: *"You have heard it said, 'Love your neighbor,' which means only the people who believe as you do."*

"The menu is not the meal." ~ *Alan W. Watts*

"Each star is a mirror reflecting the truth inside you."
~ *Aberjhani*

"This is why I speak to them in parables: Though seeing, they do not see; though hearing, they do not hear or understand." ~ *Matthew 13:13*

The word *parable* comes from the Greek *parabolē*, meaning *"comparison, illustration, analogy."* It was the name given by Greek rhetoricians to an illustration in the form of a brief fictional narrative. By speaking in parables and sharing stories Jesus was not laying down strict doctrines to be believed in and adhered to. His teachings were given as practical life lessons, which would help anyone willing to apply them to uncover their Divine connection. It makes sense that Jesus spoke metaphorically, because then his teaching would be universal and could be applied in any age, including our current time. Even with all of our advancements, his teachings reveal a very positive, practical and relevant way to live today. Metaphors are figurative, in which a word or phrase denoting one kind of object or action is used in place of another to suggest a likeness or analogy between them. A metaphor is an implied comparison. Jesus wanted his listeners to go deeper and discover the beauty of metaphysical truth.

Metaphysics is the study of things beyond the physical. It's a spiritual awareness arising within one's being and leading to the truths of life. Once you understand the symbolic way in which Jesus taught, you could then grasp the greater meaning within yourself, leading to the Abundant Life. Jesus used phrases such as, "You that have ears to hear" or, "You that have eyes to see." Most people have physical eyes and ears from which to see and hear what Jesus said, but they still did not "get" it. If you aren't ready and willing to hear from an objective state of mind the point and message of his teachings are missed completely

Metaphysical understanding reveals a deeper meaning or truth relating to the transcendent reality beyond that which is perceptible to the senses.

Metaphysical truth goes beyond the physical and literal in order to open our spiritual eyes and ears. Obviously, Jesus wanted his audience to get the true meaning of his teachings, but many could not move beyond the trappings of the material world to see the deeper level of truth. This truth leads us to a more mystical and direct knowing of God. All true spiritual paths lead to a greater awareness of God within.

"No longer do I call you servants, for the servant does not know what his master is doing; but I have called you friends, for all that I have heard from my Father I have made known to you." ~ John 15:15

Sometimes in life we have people around us who just don't "get" who we are. They only know us on an outward, physical level. Someone may know your name and converse with you, but that doesn't mean they know you. It is perfectly fine to have these kinds of superficial relationships with most people because that's the way of this world. At the corner market I speak kindly to the people who wait on me, but I don't necessarily share my every thought with them. It may not be the appropriate time to reveal what my inner guidance is teaching me. It can also create confusion when we are trying to convey a spiritual reality that works for us, but has not been revealed to the person we are involved with in our everyday experiences.

Motivation

In my days at Bible College we would go out and pass out tracts to the people on the street. The tracts were filled with Bible scriptures arranged in such a way to make people feel bad and hopefully we could get them to say a prayer of repentance with us so as to assure their ticket to heaven. We felt that it was our duty to do so or else these poor souls would go into eternal torment. There were other times I felt selfish and stayed in my dorm room in order to do my homework or rest. I never felt like I could do enough because "sinners" were everywhere.

Many of the people that were on the street really did need love and assistance just not the Bible thumping we were giving them. People deserve love and kindness, no matter who he or she is or what they have done. It would have been better if we opted to make some friendships with folks and passed out some sandwiches instead, which is what they really needed.

57

I have learned that my beliefs are sacred to me and I don't share with others unless they want me to. We are each on our path and by interfering with another persons journey is not necessarily for their highest good. Sometimes opportunities come up that do call for our inner truth to be shared. It just depends on the situations and the moments in which we find ourselves. Rather than trying to convince people on a mental level, we can share our own experience from our heart center without expecting that they must believe as we do. Everyone has a right to believe in what works in his or her own life situation. That's the respect we all owe each other. Do you want to be helpful or are you just meddling? Is your motivation love or fear?

Divine Friendship

Just as today, many people in Jesus' time wanted profoundly spiritual and deeply meaningful relationships. Our souls long for the kind of friends who understand us and can share heart to heart. We desire a more intimate spiritual understanding, leading to a greater connection and acceptance of each other. This is the level of awareness about which Jesus was teaching. It's through the idea of serving, or making ourselves (egos) small, that we can ultimately have a greater degree of understanding stemming from close friendships and spiritual intimacy.

"Do you not believe that I am in the Father (Source) and the Father is in me? The words that I say to you I do not speak on my own; but the Father who dwells in me does the works. Believe me that I am in the Father and the Father is in me; but if you do not, then believe me because of the works themselves." ~John 14:10-11

There's a common belief these days that we are eternally separated from God, who is there and wants to connect with us. The belief is that we have to act and be a certain way in order to connect with God, and that it is our sins that keep us away and apart from Source. The truth is, according to this quote, that we are always connected to God. Spirit is always there. Our lives are always intertwined with Source. Being able to sense your connection and oneness with God is the most important aspect of your spiritual life.

For many years, I felt disconnected from the Source, and my life experience was difficult because of it. The religious teachings I had received were a mix of good and bad, positive and negative. "Yes, God loves you, but the devil is after you and is trying to steal your soul." Or, "You may need to suffer for awhile in order to become worthy of God's love and grace." There were times when I felt okay with myself, but much of the time I was depressed and feeling intense shame. They taught it and I bought it... so it became my responsibility to deal with it.

Things began to change once I understood that the nature of Divinity is perfect love, and completely accepts me as I am. It was a journey and over time, I started to let go of the shame that was never really mine in the first place. I realized my inner needs were never really being fulfilled. I sought approval from people around me, as I wanted to feel connected. There was really no one who could fill the empty void I felt inside. Life was not working for me in any coherent way. That's when I finally realized my relationship with God needed a reboot. Today my life is very different. I don't even feel like that person I used to be. Now I can take a breath and sense my inner connection with Spirit anytime I need to. That's something you can't buy. It soothes me and fills the empty places inside that once haunted me. As I began to master the thoughts, which were constantly tormenting me, I arrived at an inner sense of peace, letting go of the stern god of judgment, while discovering the grace of the indwelling Presence. I am wrapped in a blanket of loving-kindness, and feel more whole than ever before. A metaphysical understanding of truth fills me from within. We can all be changed through an intimate connection with Spirit.

The Source of all life is your friend and only desires the highest good for all.

Chapter Eight

Sexuality

Jesus never said: *"It is okay for women to give birth and take care of the home but they should not have opinions and speak up for themselves."*

"Religious guilt causes people to deny their behavior even as they engage in it." ~Darrell Ray

The Middle Eastern culture was, and still is, very patriarchal. Much of the Bible reflects the influence of that early culture. Many churches have adopted these beliefs about women even today. Women cannot be ministers or spiritual leaders in many of the religions founded in the older cultures. A literal interpretation of the Bible down through the years has been responsible for women often being abused and mistreated.

It is time to stop the madness. The idea below, from Paul, has created a lot of confusion and misunderstanding.

"Women should remain silent in the churches. They are not allowed to speak, but must be in submission, as the law says." ~ 1st Corinthians 13:34

Women were not respected in ancient times because the culture basically favored men. Today, many, at least try to have a more enlightened view of men and women as being

61

equals in society. The culture of Jesus' time was very biased, but we do not need to adopt this antiquated way of life in order to gain benefit from Jesus' teachings of universal truths. Much of the Middle East still practices the suppression of women, keeping them in submission. I do not believe we need to regress and go backward in time and practice these outdated and demeaning ideas. Rather, we should continue to grow and advance to an even more inclusive society. Jesus was also not anti-woman. He had Mary, a prostitute, who followed him, and many of the men following him were upset that Jesus spoke as friendly to her as he did to them. After his resurrection, Jesus appears to women first.

We need to keep in mind that these beliefs and practices were cultural. Paul's admonition to have women, "keep silent in the churches" was based on the idea that men were stronger and needed to protect the female. Today women can hunt their own food at the grocery store and can get along quite nicely without a man around, thank you very much. Many American churches will not allow women to speak in the church or have a leadership role because of Paul's words. This is a misunderstanding of what Jesus taught. **Jesus never said** anything about women not speaking, preaching, teaching or sharing the Good News! In fact the Apostle Paul also said:

"There is neither Jew nor Gentile, neither slave nor free, **nor is there male and female, for you are all one in Christ Jesus**.*"* ~ Galatians 3:28

So, Paul was either contradicting himself with these two ideas, or maybe he was still growing in faith as he went along. Many of Paul's letters had years between them, and perhaps his understanding continued to evolve over time. Our understanding is still expanding and growing today too. We must change and adapt our belief systems to the ever-unfolding nature of the truth as it is progressively revealed to us. Paul was guided according to the customs of the time. It has taken over 1900 years for society to see the absurdity of making women second-class citizens. Women and men are spiritual equals both having unique gifts and talents to share. We all have a particular mission and perspective that the world needs.

The Beloved Community

Also from Paul's writings:

"For the kingdom of God is not a matter of eating and drinking, but of righteousness, peace and joy in the Holy Spirit." ~ Romans 14:17

The kingdom of Heaven is the beloved community that dwells here on earth. It encompasses the spiritual practice of love and kindness where everyone is accepted and treated with dignity and respect. There are no biases or prejudices anywhere to be found when living in direct connection with this spiritual kingdom. Let's look further into this idea to capture the essence of what Jesus was really calling us to.

Jesus' ministry taught about the Kingdom of God and how to access it. The Kingdom of God is not on another planet or in outer space but is the realm of pure potentiality and spiritual awareness. The above verse explains to us what the Kingdom is and is not. First, it is not a physical place or thing, but is a spiritual state of mind that denotes peace, joy and right-minded awareness. It can be experienced anywhere, at anytime, by anyone who chooses to access it. The Kingdom is within you and me. It is our birthright to fully embrace this inner kingdom, connecting us to the

Divine Intelligence. It is a higher state in which we can all live and walk this planet together in peace and prosperity. Jesus did say,

"But seek first the kingdom of God and His righteousness, and all these things will be provided for you."
~ Matthew 6:33

The Kingdom of God is contained in the eternal now, and is available to all. The stories and allegories can be interpreted in a positive way for the highest good of all. Jesus' mission was to release the captives and bring sight to the spiritually blind, no matter their race or gender. He came to heal the separation in the hearts and minds so that oneness and connection could be felt and experienced by all. The teachings of Jesus were never about controlling women or anyone else. I ask you, "What kind of 'good news' is that?"

The allegorical stories of Jesus reflected useful concepts and ideas that released people from bondage. It is time to seek the kingdom of God that represents a higher standard, which is the highest good for all and we will have whatever else we need too.

"Beloved, let us love one another, because love is from God; everyone who loves is born (fresh and new) of God and knows God." ~ 1st John 4:7

Is Sex Good Or Bad?

Why is our culture so double-minded about sex? It seems that sex sells but according to some people sex will also send you to hell. Sex is used to entice people to buy cars, burgers, pills and any number of things. Modern day marketers to create consumers that will buy their products,

64

use sexual tension. The reason they do it is because it works.

In ancient times people engaged in sex quite often too and the reason we know this is because there are so many children that came from all the sex they were having!

Is the act of sex good or is it evil? Did God create sex just for the propagation of the human race? What do our customs surrounding marriage have to do with sex? Sex has been used to shame and blame people over and over again. I was taught that sex was shameful and I was not to even think about it until I was married. It was a confusing way to grow up, to say the least. It is no wonder we cannot have an intelligent conversation with religious people about sex in our society. People are too hung up about it to deal with it in a rational way.

The Apostle Paul said it was better to "marry than to burn with lust." So was he saying, "Sex is not the highest good for you but if you must do it then get married?" So then marriage is a lesser choice than celibacy? Wow! It makes me wonder if that is why many folks that are married feel like their relationships are second rate, because they had to get married or be consumed by lust.

As a young boy I learned to look at women as body parts rather than whole people with intelligence and personalities. This was taught to me by being around other males who were my age and older. Unfortunately, many of my friends got married so they could have "legitimate sex" with body parts that turned out to be whole people with opinions, beliefs and ideas of their own.

Who Decides If Sex Is Good Or Bad?

"And I say to you: whoever divorces his wife, except for sexual immorality and marries another, commits adultery." ~ Matthew 5:32

I want to talk for a moment about the Greek word for fornication or sexual immorality, which is *porneia*. Obviously, this is where we get the word pornography. It is usually interpreted as sex outside of marriage, but I feel that is a limited understanding of the full contextual meaning of the word.

Sex is not evil, bad or wrong.
- *Sex is good because it is used to propagate the race.*
- *It can also be quite enjoyable.*

So where is the hang up? I believe that as adults each of us is responsible for what we do with our own bodies. We decide if something is right for us or not.

Porneia is the lusting for another human being to control, use or manipulate them for sexual or any addictive reasons.

Just like anything else sex is good except when it is harmful to you or another individual. Lust or all consuming desire is also connected with the concept of greed. Money is a good thing too but the lusting after it can be harmful to people. If you use, manipulate, and control others to get more money then that is your *porneia*. Food is wonderful, and we need it for our health. When you have an unhealthy desire to eat ice cream without moderation then it becomes harmful to your body. Food can also be your porn or your *porneia*.

You will reap what you have sown, and that is a universal principle. When our lives are out of balance everything is affected by it.

"For out of the heart (emotional mind) come evil thoughts, murders, adulteries, fornications, false witness, slanders."
~ Matthew 15:19

We see here other imbalances that are included with the word fornication. In other scriptures drunkenness and gluttony are mentioned too. The common theme is imbalance and extreme desires.

Adultery

Adultery is another word that has been misused. What is adultery?

"Vows broken between adults"

When a marriage breaks down and ends in divorce there is usually more going on than sexual infidelity. The vows between the two parties were broken long before sex with another person entered the picture, though marriages can break down because of many kinds of *addictive behavior or porneia*. I believe the problem with marriage is that people many times marry for all the wrong reasons. Unfortunately, lots of people do not know the difference between lust and love. A little lust or physical attraction can be healthy and positive. Again, it is the extremes that get people into trouble.

Jesus never said anything about not going to heaven because you ate too much or fooled around a little too often. These imbalances will keep you from entering the kingdom of God within you, which is a happy and peaceful state of being, especially if you don't resolve the underlying issues. I myself had to make peace with food, sex and money because if I didn't I would never be a happy and fulfilled person. It is an ongoing discipline to work to balance the physical appetites that can easily get out of control.

"I have the right to do anything," you say - but not everything is beneficial. "I have the right to do anything" - but I will not be mastered by anything."
~ 1 Corinthians 6:12

"Moderation in all things." ~ Aristotle

Life is about self-mastery and I cannot be happy until I am able to bring a sense of balance to everything I do.

Homosexuality

Jesus never said one word about homosexuality being a sin! He did not command same sex people not to marry if they chose to. In fact, he did not command heterosexuals to marry either. Marriage is a cultural issue plain and simple. It is a tradition that has been carried forth since the early stages of our human culture. I am not saying marriage is bad, but I am also not saying that marriage in and of itself is always good. It all depends on what you make of it. You are the deciding factor on whether your marriage is a positive experience or not. Just because you get married does not necessarily mean you will live "happily ever after." My wife and I have been married for well over 30 years. We were two different people that had to learn how to grow together in an optimal way. Being married can be a great experience if you are intentional about it. It will teach you so much about yourself that you can't learn any other way. Because it is a cultural issue, gay

68

people have just as much right to enter into marriage, as does anyone else.

Several years ago I had the experience of having a gay man attend our church. At the time I was opening up to the idea that God was bigger than my preconceived ideas up to that point. Instead of condemning him, I sought to understand. This subtle shift made a huge difference in how I related to this young man. His name was Tim and he shared with me that from an early age he was attracted to boys rather than girls. If that was true, then his attraction was natural because he was born that way. We had many discussions during the time as I was giving him spiritual counseling. At that time there were almost no churches that he could attend and be accepted as a gay man.

Since that time, I have come to know hundreds of men and women that were born with a same sex attraction. It has also been my honor and privilege to perform several same sex marriages once it became legal in my state. Gay people are just like heterosexuals, they want to be happy and share their life with someone they love.

This same idea is also carried throughout the rest of the New Testament including Paul's writings. We can choose to live in whatever way we choose and God loves us unconditionally, because we are God's kids. We just may not be very happy along the way. I am still loved no matter what I do or don't do. The inner Kingdom of happiness comes when I can make peace with my own "porneia" or *addictive behavior*, whatever that may be.

"I have a right to do anything I want." ~1 Corinthians 6:12

The problem comes when I overdo something and harm others or myself in the process. That is the essence of

Jesus' teachings, to master your mind and body and to create a society of people that only chooses activities that reflect the highest good for all! If God is all good and all loving, and God is the force behind all creation, then any activity or action or belief or feeling we have as humans, who are divinely inspired, that doesn't harm the rest of creation is also divinely inspired.

If gay people are loving toward themselves and loving others and not harming other people through their relationships and experiences, then there is no reason or defense in the Bible against that relationship and life experience.

God created gay people and they didn't choose that life.

All the scriptures in the New Testament that have been viewed, as "homosexuality is wrong" are actually talking about lust and extreme passions, not two people that genuinely love each other. I have met lots of people over the years that condemn gay people but many of them live in lust for money, sex and power. I really think it is time to stop condemning others and begin to look at our own lives. It is the religious persona that will keep you from fully experiencing the kingdom of God, not whom you love!

How can you think of saying, 'Friend, let me help you get rid of that speck in your eye,' when you can't see past the log in your own eye? Hypocrite! First get rid of the log in your own eye; then you will see well enough to deal with the speck in your friend's eye. ~Luke 6:42

Thankfully God is not keeping a scorecard about anybody's errors and mistakes.

Jesus said, "You who are without sin (errors) can cast the first stone."

Any takers? I didn't think so.

Chapter Nine

John 3:16

Jesus never said: *"God was so disgusted with the world that he had to do something."*

"For God so loved the world that he gave his only begotten son that whosoever believes would not perish but have everlasting life" ~ John 3:16

John 3:16, more than any other scripture, has been used to try to convict people for their sins and the guilt of being human. It's seen at many baseball games and heard from the shouting evangelists on the street corners. Some preachers have caused people to feel especially bad about their lives, emphasizing a negative connotation of this verse through the use of the word perish. But is that what this verse really says? Let's break it down and examine it a little closer to see what we can glean from this oft-quoted Bible verse.

For God soooooo loved the world...(Can you see where the real emphasis is?) God loves the world and love is its own motivation. From this premise we can read the rest of the verse more clearly. "That he gave..." - love gives and gives what is needed. God gave a Son to the world for a specific purpose, to express that higher love and invite people to also become a loving expression in the world too. The next line uses the word *perish,* and many people get confused.

To perish speaks of the idea of suffering, to experience loss, or to be separated from.

People suffer much of the time because they do not allow love to rule their lives. Jesus wanted to reveal the true nature of God as loving-kindness because love and kindness is what frees us from suffering.

Suffering can be one of our greatest teachers if we let it. But suffering is not our goal. It's simply a teacher along the pathway to wholeness. By turning to a positive view of God, we can eliminate many of the roots of our suffering. The belief that God is a torturer of lost souls and delights in sending people to hell, creates a lot of suffering in the world. Our task is to find ways to live in harmony with our own inherent divinity and find release from suffering. The state of suffering keeps us in a downward spiral of fear and dread.

Because of the negative focus in our culture today, people suffer from a plethora of mental and psychological ills. Many minds are filled with unrealistic expectations and false beliefs, which keep them bound to the status quo. Mental anguish is released when you completely forgive yourself and others. You can then achieve a sense of freedom from these mental and emotional attachments.

"No, I tell you; but unless you repent, you will all likewise perish (suffer)." ~ Luke 13:3

You can never really break a bad habit. You must replace it. Suffering comes because of the way in which you think about your life. You stay in this unpleasant state of suffering, stuck in a repetitive pattern that unconsciously works against you. You become a self-fulfilling prophecy of your negative mental patterns when you refuse to think in new ways.

The word *repent* in the Greek language is *Metanoia,* which means *to change your mind and go in a different direction.*

The ministry of Jesus was all about changing people's minds, which is how they could change their behaviors. You and I cannot change unless we do so at the root level of thinking. True repentance is not about thinking the same thought over and over again but expecting a totally different outcome. When you change your perspective and point your mind in a new and positive direction then you discover a different reality.

Teknon and Huios

In John 3:16, the Greek word for Son is the word *Huios* and is pronounced *wee-os.* This Greek word tells us about the uniqueness of Jesus, the Son of God, as being enlightened and a model of what human beings could become. We are Sons and Daughters of God, unique beings with the same potential as Jesus or any other enlightened being.

Another Greek word for Son in the Bible is *Teknon,* and means a child. What is the difference? In the ancient Jewish culture a boy is considered a child or *Teknon* until the age of 12 and then he would become an apprentice to his father to learn the family business. The Jews celebrate the Bar Mitzvah in honor of their young son's arriving at this stage of life. Interestingly, Jesus first appeared in the Temple when he was 12 years old, probably experiencing his own Bar Mitzvah.

Through time the son learns the secrets of the family trade and grows to become a co-equal with his father in the business. At the age of 30 he is then considered a joint owner of the family business and has all the rights and privileges of his father. In those days you also had to be 30 years old to be a priest or a king. The ancient people were more respectful of a person's maturity when you were at this age. Jesus was 30 years old when he began his ministry as well. His uniqueness had to do with his spiritual maturity.

Jesus apprenticed with the Father within (Source) and grew to become the Christ, or the anointed one. We are all *Teknons,* or children of God, who are to become a *Huios*, a mature Son or Daughter of God. Jesus was part of the first fruits of many of these *Huios* that were to come, and served the real purpose of being an example we could all follow. He was sent as a pattern, model and example that we could copy and emulate. God was saying to us, "here is what unconditional love looks like in physical form, and what you all have the potential to become." Thus the scripture, "This is my beloved Son *or huios* in whom I am well pleased, hear him."

Only Begotten?

Another idea that is often taught is that Jesus is the "only" offspring of God. The Greek word for *only begotten* is *monogenes* and is better translated as "unique" or "one of a kind". You add this to the thought of Jesus being a *huios* or mature Son of God then we see a clearer picture of what is being said. All of us are children of God but there are a few that have grown up and demonstrated what being a fully mature Son or Daughter of God is. We are all unconditionally loved; some are more mature in their acceptance of love and then living fully in that love than

75

others. This is really good news because that means we all have the potential to grow and mature in our spirituality.

Belief Is Total Trust

Another aspect of John 3:16 is the concept of belief in God or "trust in the positive." To believe in something you have to trust in it. How can we trust a God with an anger management problem who might get upset over our human ways and send us to a fiery pit because we did not accept the right religion in the proper way in the right church?

The nature of God is love and, therefore, cannot be anything non-loving. The love found in Jesus' teaching is unconditional. There is no greater love than this thought of "no conditions."   Sometimes human beings love according to certain conditions and, "If you act in a particular way and please me I will love you back." Divine love has no such conditions. You are absolutely loved and cherished as a being that has value and worth. You have the same capacity to love and the same value as Jesus did in the eyes of Divinity!

When the woman caught in adultery was brought before Jesus according to the law of that time, she was supposed to be stoned to death. Instead, Jesus told them, "You without sin (error thought) can cast the first stone." No one did. She had no accusers because everyone watching had made mistakes in their lives. The culture of the time was riddled with fear, shame and guilt, which is why the laws were so harsh.

Jesus was teaching a better way. That of forgiving and accepting people as they are, and nurturing them so they can grow into happy, fulfilled beings of intrinsic value and worth. Needy people are usually needy because they desire to be loved and appreciated. Lots of people are living without kindness in their lives, which causes them unhappiness of all kinds and they may not have had anyone to model for them a life of abundant joy. If your spirituality is not applicable to all people then what good is it? Jesus not only talked about how to live the abundant life, he also demonstrated it through his actions.

This is such an important point to get!

Jesus Came To DEMONSTRATE The Way That Leads To A Happy And Fulfilling Life!

Jesus did talk about being the *Way*. He is the way of peace, love, hope, joy, kindness, giving and all that is good! Jesus did not come to be the way of religion to bind people to strict doctrines that produce a one-way street mentality. That kind of "One Way-ism" is the antithesis of the teaching Jesus came to share. He showed us the way back to the Father (point of origin). We all came from the same one place and we will all return to it too.

*"The dust **returns** to the ground it came from, and the **spirit returns** to **God** who gave it. ..."*
~ Ecclesiastics 12:7

77

Chapter Ten

One Way-ism

Jesus never said: *"I am the ONLY way to God."*

"I am the way, the truth and the life and no one comes to the Father but by me." ~ John 14:6

"We accept what we think we deserve."
~ Stephen Chboski

Jesus never said," I am the "*only way*"; though many seem to automatically insert the word *only* into this Bible verse. Jesus shows the way and as we follow his teachings we discover the way of love that leads us back to the Father (Source). We find God when we open to that source of love within us.

"Truly I tell you, anyone who will not receive the kingdom of God like a little child will never enter it."
~ Mark 10:15

The nature of a child is innocence and curiosity, and being open and receptive to an experiential way of living in the world. It is a fresh state of mind that causes you to trust life fully and be born anew in each and every moment. It is not the fear of God's wrath that causes us to enter into the Kingdom. It's the opening of a tender heart that is willing to make room for God's unconditional love. That is "The

Way" to find God within as our true source. Jesus told us to learn from him and become open in mind and spirit by following his example. You discover the real value and worth of a human being by uncovering your own divine potential. When your own true value is revealed you can also see it in others.

"Love God with all your heart, soul, mind and strength and love your neighbor as you love yourself."
~ Mark 12:29-30

Jesus told us to make the law of love our priority because love is the only safe way to use our minds to create a positive life. Love is inclusive and non-judgmental and is the only power that can free your mind from the damaging effects of negative thinking.

Judgmental thinking is a mindset that can bring harm to the body, mind and spirit of the individual doing the judging. Judging others actually hurts you more than it hurts the person you judge. Being non-judgmental is a higher way in which to think and use the mind. It takes lots of energy and time to judge and label others.

"Come to me all those that carry heavy burdens and I will give you rest." ~ Matthew 11:28

When Jesus uses the personal pronoun "I", he was speaking as the Universal Christ. The Christ lives in all of us, and when we rest in that awareness, peace is the effect. Jesus was calling us inward to uncover our natural state beyond the physical world.

How would you feel if you let your mind rest more in a calm state of awareness and trust? Your mind is not really made to think harsh or violent thoughts, but is meant to be

79

a holding tank of creative spiritual energy. This energy can be used to empower and transform your life. We all contain this creative power and we already use it every day. So many people use their divine creative energy to hold themselves and others in a state of lack and limitation. Newton's Law states: "For every action, there is an equal and opposite reaction." Positive vibes create positive results as negative vibes create negative results. Whatever energy you put out is what you will get back. It is the law...

"I have come that you might have life and have it more abundantly." ~ John 10:10

By living the way Jesus taught and modeled we gain spiritual energy and can live a higher quality of life. The abundant life is a life filled with greater meaning and purpose.

Most people think of eternal as being without end, but actually the words *eternal life*, which is *aionian zoe* in the Greek, are defined as the *quality of life* rather than the quantity. It is a higher state of being rather than the length of a life. Souls continue on without end, but eternal life is the state or quality in which you experience your life without end. Living forever in a state of suffering is not the Divine plan for us and would not be very pleasant. Living in the Kingdom, the state of peace and joy is what we can all experience when we see it is possible.

You have a continuous flow of life inside you but you cut yourself off from it because of your mental thinking habits. A free flow of energy comes surging through when you finally release all blocks to it. We block the positive life energy with our many assumptions and narrow-minded thinking. When you are thinking about yourself or others in critical ways, then your energy becomes stuck.

"We are transformed by the renewing of our minds."
~ Romans 12:2

Transformation takes place when you allow your mind to exist in a calm and peaceful space. The real meaning of these teachings is that God is love, and is continually expressing love to all of creation! The cause of all suffering is a lack of love. Jesus tells us to change our minds and learn *new ways* of being, which is called the Kingdom of God. It is time for each of us to understand the true meaning of Jesus as *the way shower of loving kindness.* God loves all of us as his (or her) children, and has sent us to be examples of how to heal the world and bring a full cup of joy to this Earthly plane. In the process, we can alleviate much of the suffering in the world. The real mission of Jesus was to heal the suffering, not add to it through outdated beliefs, which only serves to alienate people. The biggest healing needed is in the thought patterns of the mind.

We must see divinity in a new and more expansive light rather than from a one-way mentality that excludes anybody that is different.

Chapter Eleven

Sinners

__Jesus never said:__ "You are all natural born sinners that are destined for hell."

"Self-worth comes from one thing – thinking that you are worthy." ~ Wayne Dyer

Your perspective on life comes from the cage you were held captive in." ~ Shannon L. Alder

Nowhere in the New Testament does it say that we are born into the world as sinners. What? Is that true?

__Jesus never said__ we were born sinners. Not one time! It does not appear anywhere in the New Testament.

When you look into the eyes of a newborn baby, you do not see sin. You see pure innocence looking back you. When I beheld the face of my children when they were born, I was deeply moved. How could anyone ever call a baby a sinner?

Yet many churches teach the idea that we are born into the world as sinful creatures that desperately need saving from our wickedness. Other churches say there is an age of accountability at which time we automatically become "sinners" ...around the ages of 8 to 10 years old. But

82

children are only reflecting back what society and culture teach and model to them. Children are born into the world perfectly innocent, with unlimited potential inside of each one.

When I was a child of about 10 years old, I went to a revival where a shouting evangelist was preaching about how hot hell was and that I could possibly be going there soon because I was so bad. At that age the worst thing I remember doing was taking a cookie from the cookie jar when Mom wasn't looking. I may have fought a little with my siblings, but on the whole I was a pretty good kid. After the evangelist spoke, I felt so bad I began to have nightmares about my "sinful condition". Here is what actually happened:

A Problem Was Created And Then A Solution Was Offered For That Problem.

It was a sales pitch, and I fell for it hook, line and sinker. Yes, they were well meaning people who were just doing what they had learned to do. I don't believe they had malicious intent. They were only doing what they thought was right in their minds. However, I did not even think in terms of sin until the idea was introduced to me. I was not a "bad" person until they "sold me" on the idea.

Many people perform certain rituals without any real mindfulness or awareness of why they do it. Traditions can be passed down for centuries without questioning. It reminds me of the story of the young woman who would cut off both ends of a ham and threw away the pieces before she would put it in the oven. She stated that her mother taught her to do this and that is why she kept doing it. Somewhere back in her family lineage a great grandmother began cutting off the ends of the ham because her pan was too small! That's how traditions are continued down through the ages without people ever questioning why.

"All have sinned and fallen short of the glory of God."
~ Romans 3:23

Notice that it *does not* say we were born as sinners, but simply that we have all sinned. The word sin in the New Testament is made to sound evil and corrupt, but the word actually means to *"miss the mark"* or to *"make an error"*. That is all it really means. We have all made errors in life from time to time. It's mostly unintentional, not coming from some depraved uncontrollable nature. Sometimes we just make a mistake or err in judgment as we go about living life. It happens. Most people are not out to intentionally hurt others. Even sadism is learned behavior picked up from some adult who had a load of guilt. Guilt and manipulation are the real errors we need to heal.

If you really want to overcome sin, do not envision yourself as a sinner any longer! What you focus on and think about is what you become. Sinners are created by religious guilt and fear, not by God. "God does not make any junk!" The heavy burden of guilt and shame drives a lot of people into depression, frustration and anger. We keep making mistakes and end up loathing ourselves to the point of creating an unhealthy self-image that keeps us in an unhappy state of mind.

Fear based religion tries to control the masses through negative consequences. Many people have lived a shame-based life because of a faulty belief system taught to them at an early age. At some point, we must reclaim our power and realize that we do not have to buy into fear and shame based thinking. If you believe God is angry with you, it could really make you a little nervous. To think that the Creator of the universe is watching every little move you make is a little self-absorbed, don't you think? God is not a voyeur watching our every movement to make sure we are not having too much fun. "God isn't an entity outside of us that is pushing a button of punishment and judgment." God is a loving nonjudgmental presence. The Divine power within us is a beautiful creative energy that gives us life and breath, and is the true source of our being.

"When I was a child I spoke as a child but when I became an adult I put away childish things." ~ I Corinthians 13:11

Now that you are an adult, you no longer want to live according to the dictates of childish fears. You want to free yourself from old and worn out ideas so you can fully embrace your true potential.

As long as you are stuck in the past, then life can be very difficult to manage. Once you see the light, so to speak, then you can let go and just be. The Divine is with you and in you always. You have never been alone. Just like the birds that are guided from within, so are you. If you continue to see yourself as a hapless sinner it affects everything you do, because you end up making choices based in fear, shame and guilt. This was my experience for many years and it was not healthy or productive.

Today, I see God in myself and in everyone. I constantly look for the good in people and choose to believe in a positive view of God and the Bible. Once you release the negative perception of divinity the whole Universe comes alive and is your friend. It doesn't mean you won't ever have a challenging day, but when you do, you can just accept it for what it is and know God is not angry with you or on the verge of punishing you for some sadistic reason.

85

Jesus Never Used Guilt Or Manipulation

Using guilt to manipulate people is not a new idea. Dictators of all the ages have used fear and guilt to their advantage to keep people in line. Adolph Hitler, as well as many others, was an expert in manipulation. We are no more brilliant than these dictators when we endeavor to control people through shame and guilt. Guilt is based in fear, not love. Jesus never wanted the kind of spirituality that threatens people with hellfire and eternal torment. Many preachers have said, "Jesus loves you, but you're going to hell if you don't repent!" This is like an abusive husband who beats his wife for not doing what he wants. This is not the loving Presence of God that Jesus spoke about. If it were, it would mean Jesus believed that guilt and fear are greater motivators than love. The nature of love is defined as unconditional, and that means no conditions.

The teachings of Jesus lead us into our true nature of genuine care and kindness. The actual nature of God is total love, acceptance and forgiveness. The word in the Bible for Divine Love is *Agape, meaning "having a realization of the true value and preciousness of a person."* "Love never fails" and love always wins out in the end. It is the greater way that Jesus taught and it is the only way to know God because God is the very essence of love, as opposed to guilt, fear or manipulation.

"Judge not unless you want to be judged." ~ Matthew 7:1

When you judge someone you are actually judging yourself. You recognize a flaw in the other person that you also have. That's why it's so familiar to you, *"mmm... I've seen this somewhere before."* The same measuring tape you apply

86

to another is also being applied to you. Whatever energy you put out is also coming back to you.

When Jesus said to "judge not" he was referring to the idea of *condemnation*. In other words, don't condemn people. It is the continual condemnation of others that creates all the chaos and confusion in the world. What would our world look like without condemnation? What if people could be free to live in peace without judgment or ridicule from others?

John Lennon wrote these powerful lyrics, "Imagine no hell below us and no religion too, and imagine all the people living life in peace." This is what Jesus really taught, and others are beginning to teach today. Can you imagine a world beyond guilt and shame where people are accepted for who they are? Can you envision a world where spirituality is free of bias and everyone is allowed to think for himself or herself? This world already exists for those who truly live the universal spirituality that Jesus talked about.

In the traditional sense, there is no "heaven" above us. Heaven is ours to claim right here and right now. It is the gentle awakening of the heart to an unconditionally loving Presence we call God. It's the joyous experience of discovering the true nature of divinity within you.

Are you ready to drop all your judgments, labeling and condemnation, and fulfill your natural God given potential?

Chapter Twelve

Non-Judgment Day!

Jesus never said: "Is that your final answer?"

"Stop judging according to outward appearances; rather judge according to righteous judgment." ~ *John 7:24*

"In its highest form, not judging is the ultimate act of forgiveness." ~ *John Kuypers*

There is the belief that God is going to judge every one of us in the hereafter or in the "last days". It's like a game show, where we are penalized if we do not give the correct response. "Is that your final answer?" "I'm sorry, but you must go to hell and suffer for eternity now because you gave the wrong answer."

I have a question about that....

Why did Jesus tell us specifically, "*not to judge people*?"

As mentioned in the last chapter, when Jesus said "don't judge" literally it means *don't condemn*. The other word for judgment in the Greek is *krisis* and is translated as the idea of *critiquing or a moment of decision*. ***Jesus never said*** *anything* about a final judgment that included *condemnation and damnation*. The Greek word *krisis* is the root word for our English word *crisis*. Jesus was bringing people to a moment of decision. He wanted them to make a definite choice about whether or not they wanted to let go of their false personae and live in harmony with God, or continue the same ways of being that kept getting them into trouble. Our old ways of living in the world can teach us about what we don't want and that is important to know and understand. Once you see clearly what it is that's not working for you, you can make a new choice and go in a different direction altogether and that's what a crisis can be if you use it in a positive way. If you are *"in crisis"* then you need to consider what you need to do in order to find that better way. A crisis does not have to lead you to something bad. It can actually become the catalyst for a new life of blessing and fulfillment.

Jesus mentioned the concept of the "last day" and how experiencing a critique of your lessons learned could be helpful. Many times he put the word *righteous* in front of the word judgment, which means, *right minded or right thinking*. Jesus was showing us the error of our thinking and how, by changing our minds, we could save ourselves a lot of trouble and self-inflicted pain.

You Can Make A New Choice By Changing Your Thinking!

If Jesus taught the idea of non-judgment, then obviously *krisis* does not include condemnation, or Jesus would have been contradicting himself. We need to remove the idea of fear from "the last judgment" if we want to understand what it truly means. Jesus was not speaking about some kind of *last day barbecue pit* where people would be thrown into burning flames and tortured mercilessly because they did not attend the "right" church! That's strictly a human trait called holding a grudge!

89

The last day analogy metaphorically refers to the time right before the end of your life cycle, when you will experience a *critique or review* of how you lived your life and what lessons you learned. It's not about being condemned or the damnation of your Soul, but a simple revealing of what was learned and how much growth occurred.

In most near death literature people report experiencing a *life review*. Millions of people have been resuscitated and shared their experience of what it was like to transition into the next realm of existence. The last thing you will do concerning the life you have lived is to determine what you learned and how much wisdom you gained.

This is what life is really about, to learn the lessons as we go along, and graduate to a more peaceful state. The "last day" is simply a moment of reflection when you get to review how it went and then to make new choices in the next chapter of your immortal life.

Unfortunately, the description of the Last Judgment, as given in the Gospels, has been used to terrify, and thus compel people to unite with the church... or else! In this day of enlightenment people are not so easily led or driven by fear. They ask for wisdom and understanding. As you seek light concerning the idea of judgment, then you learn that judgment is really a matter of Divine Law. You'll find that every departure from Divine Law causes you to suffer, not in some future time of great tribulation, not in a terrifying judgment after death, but in this life, here and now.

What is the Divine Law? It's the universal, self-corrective nature in us that tells us when we are hitting, or missing, the target. It's the innate knowing of what is positive versus negative in our experience, and this knowing can be quickened and cultivated for optimal living if we use it right. Quickening does not come by the study of external things, but by concentrating the mind on the Christ within.

"You, then, why do you judge (condemn) your brother or sister? Or why do you treat them with contempt? For we will all stand (now) before God's judgment (corrective) seat.

It is written: As surely as I live, says the Lord, every knee will bow before me; every tongue will acknowledge God, (Divine law).

So then, each of us will give an account of ourselves to God. (Self-responsibility & life review)

Therefore let us stop passing judgment (condemnation) on one another. Instead, make up your mind not to put any stumbling block or obstacle in the way of a brother or sister.

I am convinced, being fully persuaded in the Lord Jesus, that nothing is unclean in itself. But if anyone regards something as unclean, then for that person it is unclean."
~Romans 14:10-14

Non-Judgment Day

According to these scriptures, judgment is not something out in the future, but a present tense reality. We stand before the all-corrective nature of Divine Law that already dwells within each one of us. When we miss the mark, this inward law of being helps us to self-correct by revealing to us what we need to know through a reflection of our world and the circumstances around us.

91

Judgment means critiquing and correcting. We are all responsible for our actions, including everything we say and everyone we label with our words. A future judgment would not be very helpful because we would not have learned anything. The key to learning is to see your mistakes as you go along, and correct and work with them to bring about a better outcome.

In the Old Testament the famed Ark of the Covenant contained within it the *mercy seat.* Jesus reminded us that if you show mercy you then receive mercy. The judgment (critiquing) seat is the mercy seat acting through Divine Law! If we judge others we will also be judged with the same measuring stick. The word of God, or Divine Law, works with each of us individually. We already have it inside of ourselves because that is where it has always been and is most needed.

Jesus was a pattern of unconditional love, showing us how to live an enlightened life in the world. We, too, are to be examples of this divine life by living in accordance with what we have learned along the way.

Nothing is unclean or impure in and of itself. It depends on our individual perception and how we view the world around us. If you judge something as bad then it becomes a bad thing to you. If you decide to see something as positive then for you it will become a positive experience. It all depends upon your beliefs, perceptions and the choices you make about how you want to live your life and interpret the world around you.

Jesus was teaching Non-Judgment Day every day. If you don't judge or condemn, then you won't, in return, be judged or condemned. The judgment comes back to us like a boomerang. If you throw it out there, you get it back!

You reap what you sow in every moment, tempered with mercy and grace. God is in love with you and only wants to do you good. Receive the grace of this divine blessing, and know that God is for you and not against you!

Chapter Thirteen

Healing Savior

Jesus never said: *"God wants to save almost everybody, accept for those he will destroy in the end-times."*

"These things I have spoken to you that my joy may be in you, and that your joy may be full." ~ John 15:11

"For the Son of man is come to seek and to save that which was lost." ~ Luke 19:10

What does it mean to be saved? What was Jesus actually talking about when he used the words *saved* and *salvation*?

I remember when I first attended a little neighborhood church down the street from where I lived as a child. They had converted a large apartment house into a church meeting space and invited all the folks from the neighborhood to come. The people were very nice but they seemed mainly interested in my being saved. In fact, they were very insistent that I "find Jesus" (I didn't know he was lost!) before it was too late.

At some point I followed their direction and did all the things I was supposed to do in order to ensure I had my ticket to heaven. I attended church nearly every time the door was open. On any given Sunday morning, Sunday evening and Wednesday night you could find me on the front row listening very intently to what the preacher had to say.

Wanting To Fit In

As I look back on that time in my life, I can see that I was looking for love and acceptance so I accepted their teaching to feel a sense of belonging. I was a shy person that needed validation. I remember once as a young teen I caught a pop up fly ball in a church soft ball game. I was standing way in the back of the field and I had to run and catch the ball without a mitt. The church youth leader was so impressed that he sang my praises to everyone who would listen. It is amazing how I still remember that experience after all these years. But, that is the kind of validation I needed at the time, to feel that I had value in someone's eyes. Many people come to religion wanting to find acceptance and to get a sense of belonging and connection. We often give our power away to almost anyone that will love and accept us. Their acceptance of me was based upon whether or not I accepted their belief system.

I now believe that the Divine loves and accepts all of us just as we are! What if the mission of Jesus was not to "rescue" the world but to empower people to heal themselves and others? This idea could change everything that you have heard about who Jesus was!

Savior And Healer

According to the Greek language, Jesus was called the *Soter,* which has frequently been translated as Savior. *Soter* can also be translated as Healer! Healer is a more useful translation, especially if you read the gospels and see that Jesus' primary mission was really about healing and wholeness.

A Soter was a Greek God with special powers, unique gifts and talents. So what special powers did Jesus possess and what did he do and demonstrate more than anything else? He came to heal the hearts and minds of the people he shared with. Many times they would be physically healed, also. That is how healing works: first, heal the inner, and then the outer follows suit.

Jesus is the Great Healer, which means that humanity was in need of recovery from the sense of separation. People have been so beaten down by the world that they lose their sense of connectivity and oneness. The prevailing theology at the time of Jesus was completely based in fear and shame. It is difficult to believe that you are a child of God and belong to a spiritual kingdom of joy, peace and love if you are afraid of some remote and distant divine judge. Jesus came to heal our perception about God and about ourselves. We are all created as divine beings and we have creative abilities and talents. Unfortunately, many people have used their talents for battle and warring rather than healing and serving.

The word *Soter* was taken from Greek mythology and represents the idea of a Divine being. Zeus and Dionysus were both called Soters. They were Olympian Gods, both with unique powers and abilities, which separated them from being mere mortals. This is the same word they used for Jesus as the Healing Savior. As we read the gospels, we see Jesus' unique gifts were about healing the separation between God and humanity. He also taught healing between people, countries and nations.

A Savior is "one who delivers people and brings them out of harm's way." They assist others in finding safety, health, healing and wholeness. It also includes, in this case, the recovery of the true self. Jesus came to help humanity connect with their true essence of divinity. He demonstrated how to do this. He spoke of joyous principles, which opened the door to living a happy and fulfilled life. The idea Jesus used of being "lost" is simply that we have gotten ourselves stuck somewhere in the unconsciousness of our own minds. The "lost" mind keeps us separated from the deeper connection and communion with the inner Presence.

How Are We Saved?

The two Greek words for the word salvation and saved are *soteria* and *sozo* and both of them contain the idea of *wellness and wholeness*. Jesus as a Healing Savior desired to love and lead people into a state of wholeness and wellness. When Jesus spoke about people being saved he was sharing with them a way of life that leads to an inner awakening. He was literally talking about a state of wellbeing. To be saved means that you apply the spiritual teachings and allow a calming peace to settle within you. You are acutely aware of the loving kindness that gently enfolds your life and you experience joyous awakenings on a regular basis. You have found a holistic way to live in a world of conflict and struggle and you are no longer buying into the critical, stressful sense of life that many people are caught up in today.

It is possible to gain freedom from error thinking (sin) and experience a way of living that is healthy, intelligent and rewarding. When you use the universal principles in your life they help heal your fears and conflict-based thinking.

I have talked to folks over the years that believed they were on God's good list because they said the proper prayer yet performed the right ritual; yet there was not much peace in their lives, and the doctrine they adhered to contradict the peaceful life that Jesus promised. Our healing comes as we let go of our prejudices and pain so we can be inwardly healed of our misperceptions and mistaken identities.

Salvation, or holistic healing, then becomes a process of inner transformation through spiritual practice. Because we live in a constantly changing environment we must continually renew ourselves in spirit, mind and body.

You Must Be Born Again?

Only one time do the words "born again" appear in the Gospels, and it is only in the King James Version of the Bible in John 3:3. It is the story of Nicodemus questioning Jesus about what he should do to find this wholeness and wellbeing. Jesus compared it to being like the wind and how we can feel its effects but do not know where it comes from. Jesus did not command that we have to be born again to enter heaven when we die, but rather to be born anew, or literally, to be refreshed. Human existence can be stressful and each of us needs a spiritual practice that allows us to renew ourselves on a regular basis. We all need the breeze of spirit to move through our lives and refresh us.

Just as a computer will become fragmented after a while and will not function properly if not rebooted and defragged on a regular basis, so you and I can also become tired, stressed and fragmented and need a reboot. We need to rekindle ourselves spiritually and regain our sense of connection to life. Without a good solid connection we are not functioning at an optimal level. The truth is we are born anew in every moment. As we take in a fresh new breath we can rediscover the Sacred Presence inside us and experience peace and rest for the mind and body.

Jesus never said, *"You must accept me (Jesus) as your own personal Lord and Savior."*

You will not find these words anywhere in the New Testament! However, many people repeat these words over and over again, thinking this is the ultimate message of Jesus. Actually, the gospel is a universal message that can assist anyone in finding and recovering the state of wellness and wholeness (salvation).

The Kingdom of God is a present reality and not a place to go in the afterlife. Everyone goes to what has been called heaven or the spiritual dimension when they leave the body. After all, we are spiritual beings and it makes sense that is our true abode. It is not a reward for saying the right prayer at the right church. In the physical world we have a body and we interact with all the things that make up the physical world. In the spirit world we will interact the way that spirits do. We already have our ticket to heaven and it is called death (state of transition) and it comes to each and every one of us. We will all transition to that world when our time comes.

Remember, Jesus is the example we can follow into a greater sense of peace and wellbeing. We do not have to worry about the afterlife! Jesus did not speak of it in the way it is presented in many churches. Though having a positive concept of heaven as discussed in chapter four can help us to gain more clarity and understanding.

"That if you confess with your mouth the Lord Jesus and believe in your heart that God has raised Him from the

dead, you will be saved. For with the heart one believes unto righteousness, and with the mouth confession is made unto salvation." ~ Romans 10:9-10

The above verse seems to give a formula for salvation or the idea of being healed and brought into wholeness. Why is it important to profess with your mouth and believe in your heart about Jesus as Lord? Interestingly the Greek word for *Lord* is *kurios* and describes someone who has achieved mastery or obtained a Master's level of spiritual maturity. Jesus in the Bible is said to be Lord of Lord's and King of King's (though it uses the masculine terms the feminine is implied because God does not prefer one gender over another). Who are these Lords, Kings and Queens? They are you and I, for, as we believe in Jesus' potential then that means we can have it too.

"Very truly I tell you, whoever believes in me will do the works I have been doing, and they will do even greater things than these, because I am going to the Father." ~ John 14:12

Jesus was not claiming Lordship to put himself in a class by himself. He was demonstrating mastery so we could see how to become masters too. We must believe in our hearts rather than our heads because that is where the growth must take place. We believe that he was raised from a physical consciousness to a divine life consciousness. Most people walk around in a death like state of unconsciousness feeling disconnected from the Higher Power. Jesus stated very plainly that, "I Am the resurrection", even before he died. He was already living in a raised state of consciousness and aliveness. That is what he wants us to believe in; that we can live in a much higher consciousness than the limitations we have placed on ourselves.

"For with the heart one believes unto righteousness" (right mindedness) that brings us into a state of reconciliation with our higher spiritual good. We must believe, or live, from our heart center, and profess and affirm our "salvation," which is the idea of wholeness. We need to affirm the good that is within us in order to more fully experience it. Affirmations can help move us toward a healthy state of being. Knowing our true essence as spiritual beings, and affirming or *agreeing with* the truth of who we are, is what brings about the healing process that "saves" us from missing the mark of our true identity.

Jesus never said, *"I have come to give you the proper religion."*

In fact, he did not come to start another religion, or to bind people to certain beliefs, which would become another ideology that separates people from each other. He was teaching a way to live in the world that was healthy, intelligent and extremely practical. A lot of people have given up on reading the Bible because of the fearful way in which it has been taught to them and they don't want anything to do with the Bible, especially if they have only ever been condemned by the people who quote it. Through the lens of fear God becomes the frustrated parent who is always angry with his children and knows only how to punish them for their ignorant mistakes.

In reality, God is Spirit and works from the inside to connect with every one of us. The living Intelligence is in our very cells keeping us alive as the Source of all life, not because we are good or bad but because we are part of a divine creation. God is not a "guy in the sky" who exists separate from us, but as the Loving Presence that is always with us. We are made of the substance of God and

101

everyone has the potential to express the Kingdom of God, right here and now.

Together we can create the beloved community of heaven on earth. The practical message of the gospel is that we can have a happy and prosperous life here in this world (where it is definitely needed).

So I am continually in process of being saved (healed) until I obtain mastery of the spiritual, mental, emotional and physical dimensions of my life. I continue to confess and believe that Jesus became Lord of heaven (spiritual) and earth (physical), which opens the door and the way for me to follow his example into that resurrected state of being and oneness!

Now THAT is something to shoot for!

Chapter Fourteen

Divine Mind

Jesus never said: *"Only my disciples have it all figured out but not those other religions."*

"When the Spirit of truth comes, he will guide you into all the truth, for he will not speak on his own authority, but whatever he hears he will speak, and he will declare to you the things that are to come." ~ John 16:13

"Christ in you the hope of glory." ~ Colossians 1:28

The word for Christ in the New Testament means the *anointed one.* Jesus became the Christ through his own personal process of enlightenment and spiritual growth. We are all part of the collective body of Christ as Paul states in his letters. Each one of us must go through our own process of discovering our identity as part of the Christ and then maturing in our spiritual understanding of what that means. It is an experience that we partake of from within.

Through meditations, prayers and silence the spirit is filling us to receive the inner saturation of the anointing as the spiritual enlivening of our being. This inner working of spirit increases our ability to love more fully and to become more calm and peaceful. This "healing oil" seeps through the personality causing us to discover a lighter state of being. As we continue our practice of oneness with spirit we will develop and grow into a more sane and intelligent way of being. We uncover our divinity within so that we can no longer hide our light under a basket and we become a healing presence in the world.

"Do to others what you would have them do to you."
~ Matthew 7:12 (The Golden Rule)

As we begin to view each other as a part of the Christ, we can start to see our true value and worth reflected back to us. As I look at another person and treat them according to the golden rule, I am rewarded with the same energy. When I acknowledge the sacred being of others I am recognizing the true nature of humanity. Our divinity has been hidden from our egocentric minds through a misperception. Once we awaken to our spiritual nature we can see through our false identity into the reality of the living Christ within.

"The creation itself also will be set free from its slavery to corruption into the freedom of the glory of the children (Huious or mature ones) of God. For we know that the whole creation groans and suffers the pains of childbirth together until now. And not only this, but also we ourselves, having the first fruits of the Spirit, even we ourselves groan within ourselves, waiting eagerly for our adoption as sons, the redemption of our body."
~ Romans 8:21-23

The very purpose of humanity is to evolve into this higher state of awareness. All lack and misunderstanding in the world is due to our spiritual immaturity. Jesus was the model of a fully formed Christ. We are called to rise to that same expanded Christ consciousness. Today we need more role models who have embraced the greater potential of their Christ nature and choose to manifest it now.

We are seeing the evidence of this Christ awakening in the world. It may not be fully revealed yet but the hunger for change is in the air and Christ is knocking at our collective heart door asking to be released from the depths of our being. Christ is not trying to come into you in an external way. Christ is the spiritual potential that exists inside of every child, woman and man in the world. To see the divinity within your own being is the beginning of your awakening. It is the start of your transformation from a caterpillar into a butterfly, from a human being into a heavenly being.

We are in a great era of transition in our society and the world. Many of the old ways in which we did things are proving not to work any longer. Anything built on the sinking sand of outdated tradition is being questioned and new paradigms are being explored. We must be willing to question all of our paradigms in order to see if they hold up.

The challenge we face is that the old paradigm is fighting anything new with a vengeance. Many people long for the "good old days" that really never were and that can never be again, by insisting we go back to the past. Our brains tend to gloss over the past and make it look and sound better than it may have been. The old systems can be influenced from the inside and that is a positive thing to do. Many of them are breaking down so quickly that new systems need to be created so that people have somewhere to go when the old finally gives way.

Who's Driving Your Car?

In our younger years we had less thoughts and concepts filling our minds with stress-filled "to do lists". Today, we are over burdened with so many maintenance tasks we must do to keep pace that we have little time for a regular spiritual practice. However, some things may not be worth the added upkeep and time it takes to keep it going. As long as I use material things to support and assist me I am blessed. When I become enamored with cars, homes and titles so they become the end game of my existence, then that is when I can lose touch with my inner spiritual essence and power. Having the ego drive the car is like having nobody that is really accountable at the wheel.

Much of what we do is driven by guilt or perfectionism so that we perform certain actions not because we need to necessarily, but because we think it is expected of us. Our expectations are beyond what our minds were meant to handle. The remedy is to first discover what it is that we are to do for ourselves, and second, what is it the Divine Mind can do for us. Once we engage the Higher Mind (intelligence and intuition) we can let go of many fears, which have kept us bound to the past.

Who Takes Care Of The Future?

The Divine Mind takes care of the future and holds that responsibility. Just let that sink in... It is not your job to be overly concerned with what happens in the future. Regardless of the plans we need to make to prepare for things that will be coming up and for times when it is necessary for us to think ahead, what really blocks us is the constant projection into the future. The fact is, we all exist in the eternal now and must stay rooted in the present moment. Worrying, obsessing, or trying to control the future is, ironically, what blocks your future good from arriving.

The Higher Mind keeps us on track toward a bright future through the signs and synchronicities that show up in the current moment. We always have what we need when we can stay connected to our Source. The Source wants to take care of us but we need to have a relationship of total trust and surrender to the inner promptings and urgings of the Higher (Christ) Mind.

"My thoughts are higher than your thoughts and my ways are higher than your ways." ~ Isaiah 55:9

The "little mind" is responsible to keep us aware of what is happening in the moment. That is its true purpose. This awareness keeps us tuned in, and aligned with the subtle energies going on inside of us in any given moment. The "little mind" cannot easily handle more than what is currently going on without getting stressed. The Higher Mind handles the details and the connecting points that get us to where we need to be.

Let The Higher Mind Take The Lead...

Ben was living on the east coast but had been in talks about a position opening up on the west coast. He would need to be at a particular gathering on a certain day so he could meet the people who would be doing the hiring. It was in the middle of winter but he was determined to be aboard the plane and make his connecting flights to get to where he needed to go, or so he thought. On the day of departure he arrived bright and early to the airport to catch this important flight.

When he walked in to the airport he noticed that many flights were being cancelled on account of the snowstorms in the Midwest. His heart sank as he learned that his flight was also cancelled. After he left the counter he had the thought that God must be punishing him for some reason as he was just hoping for a break. Just then he also had another thought, "What if this is a sign for me that there is something better in my future?"

He took a deep breath and began to notice his surroundings and the people around him. At that instant he felt the Source within him nudging him to trust in the positive and simply turn it over to the Higher Mind. He had an urge to stop by a coffee shop and relax for a moment. After purchasing a magazine and getting a cup of coffee he sat down to regroup.

About that time Joe walks into the coffee shop and they see each other. Ben and Joe were high school friends and had not seen each other for a number of years. They talked for quite a while about old times. Joe asked Ben where he was headed before the snowstorm kept him from flying out. Ben explained his situation and Joe listened intently. Ben was looking at a marketing job that had been promised to him before his flight was cancelled. Joe spoke up and said, "What a coincidence?" "Our firm is actually looking to hire someone for our marketing department." "Are you interested," asked Joe? As it turned out this position was a perfect fit for Ben and had an even better salary than the job on the West Coast.

The Higher Mind knows when the bridge up ahead is out and where we need to make a detour or a pit stop. The Higher Mind was able to get Ben to the airport so he would "coincidently" run into Joe. Ben's frustrated and agitated little mind had to be soothed and kept in a peaceful state so that he could make the rendezvous at the right time. When we relax and go with the flow we get to where we need to be even faster. Ben could have gotten angry and stormed out of the airport and missed the opportunity. Instead he took a brief moment to align with the spirit within and centered himself. That was his way of tuning in to the Higher Mind's capacity to bring him to the right place at the right time!

The Function Of The Personality

The "little mind" of personality is not the part of us that is in charge. Its only function is to stay in the present moment and follow the guidance of the higher mind through practiced awareness. Most of our problems stem from the "little mind" trying to run the show and then getting into trouble. Without the connection to our higher mind fear becomes our only guide, and that is a limited way to live. Each day we must surrender to our inner guide in order to receive what we need. It is wonderful to know that my finite personality does not have to figure everything out. My life is on purpose and there is a plan unfolding in every moment. It does not mean that everything is fate or destiny, but rather if I first align myself with the spiritual mind then I will make all my connections on time.

What Exactly Is The Higher Mind?

The higher mind is the aspect of our selves that did not incarnate into the physical world. Like the story of the Prodigal Son it is the part of us that stayed home. We have a friend on the other side that is only interested in our highest good. This higher aspect of ourselves also has the view from the mountaintop and truly understands the bigger picture. The higher mind is also connected to a greater degree with the Divine Spirit and in a real sense is God.

God is absolute intelligence and we all contain this inner Christ brilliance inside us. We simply need to connect with it on a regular basis and trust that we are in the flow of oneness. We connect to Oneness through alignment and we cannot have any more of God than we already have. All of God is available to us at anytime. In this way life becomes a constant prayer as it says in the book of Proverbs:

"Trust in the Lord with all your heart and do not lean on your own understanding. In all your ways acknowledge Him, and He will make your paths straight."
~ Proverbs 3:5

"What, Me Worry?" ~ Alfred E. Newman

Trust is actually one of the biggest issues you will have in your life. Until your trust issues are resolved you will most likely stay living in fear. Fear is a lack of trust in Divine order. We all are trusting in something every minute of the day. The key is to completely trust in the higher good no matter what happens.

Whatever is going on in your life it is always wise to acknowledge the Lord, which means trusting that the higher Christ Mind will work anything and everything for your highest good. It is the constant surrendering to this Higher Mind that aligns us with our greatest purpose. You cannot miss whatever you need to experience if you are in a state of trusting and allowing. All circumstances can be used to bring you more of the good you desire. Everything in your life can be used to bring about a positive experience if you stay in the trusting state.

The Receiving Mind

The brain is actually a receiver that picks up on the divine ideas coming your way. When we try and use the brain to control our lives we are misusing it. We seek control but cannot have control through the brain. We try to make everything outside of us line up so we can be at peace, but it never really works because the brain is simply meant to receive. The brain's proper function is to monitor thoughts and feelings that come our way. Then the personality acts on what is received according to its perception. Analysis is good to a certain point, but over analyzing everything leads to confusion and stasis.

Stress in our lives is caused by trying to figure everything out. The constant second-guessing and projecting into the future serves only to put us in a state of struggle. By using the brain for its intended purpose we can more easily surrender to the Higher Mind. Fear is a natural part of the brain we have over stimulated with our need to control. If you need to control everything going on in your life you will not have peace. If the majority of your thoughts are about trying to control people or circumstances, you will become overly stressed and potentially diseased. People who can let go and follow their inner guidance will be lighter, healthier and far happier. The key is surrendering control to the Higher Mind.

How Do I Surrender More Deeply?

Some people have the idea that surrender is giving in to situations where we are abused and controlled. "Surrender is a defeated stance and leaves me vulnerable." "Why try?

"Life will beat me down anyhow," is an all too common belief that some people hold. The truth is actually subtler than that.

True surrender is an inner feeling of perfect alignment with the peace of God that is beyond the little mind's understanding.

Before you do anything else you want to have peace as a basis from which to live your life. Peace is the ground of being wherein the Presence of God arises. God is already inside you, and a calm sense of self keeps you resonating with divinity. This is the true point of our power; by making peace in every moment you are able to hear the guidance that is coming from within. Your brain and personality then function in harmony with the higher good that is already yours. You cannot miss this good if you will keep your peace.

To be in the now-moment is to be at peace. An old preacher said, "Your arms are too short to box with God." If you are constantly fighting with God, you will lose every time. The real "fight" is the one going on between your ears.

Becoming A Listening Presence

Our natural state of being is joyful, calm and peaceful. The reason peace does not come easily to most people is because society has trained us to fight and resist everything. We buy in to the notion of what the world tells us; that we are bad, broken and need fixing. The truth is you are not bad and you don't need to be fixed. The sense of brokenness just needs to be turned into the feeling of surrender.

We are simply focusing our energies in the wrong direction by speaking first and then trying to listen. This is the case of locking the door after the horses have already left the barn. If Divine Intelligence is talking then we must learn to hear what is being said before we engage our mouths. Most of what you really want in life is accomplished on an inner level first.

Have you ever been sitting in a restaurant and overheard a conversation going on at another table? In that moment, especially if they are soft spoken, your senses become highly attuned and you are listening with your whole being.

That's the kind of listening we need to have with which to hear the urges and promptings of inner spirit. I like to call this the "Activation of the Listening Mind." This implies a receptive mind that hears what it needs to, and then the personality can act on the revelation. It's the proper use of the brain that empowers us and that is why we have ear and eye "gates" surrounding the brain. It's our ultimate receiving device of information. Use it as it is intended and you will have very good success.

"When two or more gather together in my name (inner divine nature) I am there." ~ Matthew 18:20

When Jesus fully embraced the spirit of the Christ he experienced real oneness with this Great Intelligence that knows all things. This is the sweet spot in life and is available to all. Oneness is the idea of two or more merging with each other in a calm listening state of receptivity. You cannot understand me until you can feel and sense what I am truly feeling on the inside.

It is absolutely possible for two people to experience this state of oneness if they know how to listen intuitively. This is the aligned experience with the Christ Presence or the Higher Mind. This connected feeling of oneness produces a field of sacred energy enjoyed by all who are gathered together. I have been in this energy field many times over the years in different situations and gatherings, such as spiritual services or even a wedding. It is a healing field that uplifts everyone involved.

The Christ energy is never condemning or judgmental. The energy of condemnation will almost always feel constrictive and limiting. The loving awareness of the Christ energy connects and leads to peace filled resolution. It is the real reason for gathering in the name of the loving, joyous, calming nature of the Christ Spirit.

The Christ Mind will never guide us to harm another. **Jesus never said** anything about harming your enemies. Instead, he taught the power of oneness and agreement.

"But I say to you, love your enemies, bless those who curse you, do good to those who hate you, and pray for those who spitefully use you and persecute you."
~ Matthew 5:44

So the real question is, "How can I make an enemy my friend?" The world cannot prosper, as it should until people are willing to forgive, and to release, the current and past generations of their mistakes and errors. Peace on earth happens when peace is in us and we are focused on it. We must practice peace as if we really believed in it and truly desired it, not just flowery words, or else we are just repeating slogans and nice sayings. We live in the era of change and whatever direction the world goes in next has everything to do with what we choose to focus upon.

Put on the Mind of God and let yourself be guided to a more expanded life!

"For who has known the mind of the Lord so as to instruct him? But we have the mind of Christ."
~ *1st Corinthians 2:16*

May we all move now into a better state of being and listen for the Divine Mind.

Chapter Fifteen

State of Being

Jesus never said: *"I am the Son of God...not you."*

"Perhaps home is not a place but simply an irrevocable condition." ~James Baldwin

"Happiness is nothing but a state of mind which only your thoughts and beliefs could place you in."
~Edmond Mbiaka

Jesus answered a question posed to him by declaring, "Before Abraham was, I Am." In fact, he used this phrase throughout the gospels. The words *I Am* reflected the connected state of being that Jesus inhabited. He practiced present moment awareness and completely surrendered to whatever arose in his experience. It is not our situations or circumstances, which are the most important, but our state of being. Like Jesus, if we stay focused in the present moment, we will see our circumstances change to match our state of being.

Our primary reality is within and the world outside is a secondary reality. When Jesus said to, "seek first the kingdom of heaven" he was talking about our inner state of awareness and attentiveness. As we make this our spiritual practice then all the other things, including mental, emotional and tangible benefits will be added to us.

116

Most people are hypnotized and mesmerized by the world of form around them. They walk around in a trance, repeating patterns of behavior, which are reckless and harmful. We must return to the *I Am* state in order to awaken to the primary reality, which is within. The kingdom within is our inner state of peaceful and joyful awareness.

I AM A Garden of God

Our true dwelling is the Garden of Eden that we ran from long ago. Eden was not necessarily a literal place somewhere on the earth but is actually our true state of being. Adam and Eve are us! They tell us about our natural state, which is readily available, and our great connection to divinity. Most of us have run from our glory and hidden from our true nature of love and peace for most of our lives. We have forgotten the beautiful, innocent state we inhabited when we were born into the world as babes.

Eden in the Hebrew language means, "*place of pleasure and bliss.*" Bliss is our true home that is always nearer than our breath. Bliss and joy is the natural state of the child within you. Once you have truly stilled the mind you will realize the bliss of your inner being. This state is already contained inside of you. You do not need to go anywhere to get it because it is not outside of you. Bliss is what we are. You don't need any substances or outward stimulation to find it. This natural joy arises from the quiet space of your own soul.

Jesus was a model for us to follow. Everything he taught was not so much about bragging about his own glory, but to reveal the collective glory we have forgotten. You are a child of God with unlimited potential that you can use for good. You are a garden of God, and now is the time to reap the fruit of your garden.

"I AM the Bread of Life and whoever comes to me will never be hungry again." ~ John 6:35

Many theologians believe that Jesus is the only loaf of bread we are to partake of. The truth is, I am also the bread of life and so are you. We feed people with the energy of our words to nourish and strengthen each other. To be fulfilled we must eat more than just physical food. We need love too. Yes, love is a food and we cannot reach our potential unless we are feeding upon this nourishing manna from heaven. Love is the bread that is created and made within each one of us. It is baked in the oven of our hearts and minds through our positively focused attention.

Whenever we speak from our hearts the truth we know we are sharing the bread of life. It is living bread rather than theological concepts of the mind. The true bread worth eating comes from an enlightened mind that is directed by the heart. This is our daily bread and it is manna from the heaven within.

"I AM the door of the sheep." ~ John 10:7

Here again, what Jesus says about himself is also true of us. We are to be like open doors that the sheep can come through, and enjoy a positive energy exchange and find green pastures on which to feed. **Jesus never said** I am the fence to keep the sheep boxed in!

Religions have erected great theological fences, which have become barriers to keep many people locked up rather than allowing them to experience life on their own terms. Fortunately some of the sheep have found holes in these fences to crawl through and have discovered beautiful pastures in which to feed. We can all become a doorway that people find open and accessible as we choose to be a door that leads to all kinds of possibilities.

Be an open and allowing person that others can be around without feeling stress, pressure and unrealistic expectations coming at them. Jesus could sit with the folks living out of alignment with their own divinity and they did not feel condemned. Instead, they felt okay to share with Jesus their true thoughts and dreams, even their fears and pain. Jesus presence was very comforting and a safe place to land. It is amazing that the word *safe* and *salvation* are similar. Unfortunately, many people that claim salvation sometimes do not feel very safe to be around. May we all become a safe haven for others to be with to find healing, grace, and comfort.

"I AM the light of the world." ~ John 9:5

To have the spiritual light Jesus spoke about, we must first seek understanding and wisdom. The light is the spirit essence of the soul that shines forth from our eyes. In Revelation 1:14 we read that, "Jesus' eyes shone like flames of fire." That means he was seeing from a very enlightened state of being.

To be the light in the world means to light the way for others to follow our example. The world needs real leaders and heroes to follow, which means we must lead by example. When you overcome something in your life then you can turn around and show the person near you how you did it and you can become an inspiration to many.

"I AM the resurrection and the life." ~ John 11:25

To be resurrected we first have to *die to, or release* our ego driven negativity. We can live a life of raised consciousness when we take responsibility for our choices and decisions. It is the same idea that Jesus taught about seeds needing to fall into the earth and die and then rise from the ground as a beautiful plant. We are to bloom where we have been planted. When Jesus said "Thy will, not mine, be done" he was in total surrender. This is a place where we can be in complete agreement and harmony with God.

I AM That I AM

The story of Moses meeting the *I AM Presence* is full of great metaphysical understanding. In reality it was an inner revelation that Moses experienced. The mountain he ascended was within his own heart. He was able to communicate with the *I AM Presence* of his own being. The burning bush was his illumined spirit on fire with Divine Passion. In spite of his fear he was able to accept his mission and become the leader he was called to be.

We all have the capability of connecting with our own *I AM Presence* when we are ready. Whatever you couple with the words *I AM* is very powerful. Jesus never said anything derogatory about himself. He knew the power of his words and chose to speak from that *I AM Presence*. We need to follow his example and learn the language of empowerment. When I say, "I can't" I am limiting the greater one within me. When I say, "I am a loser" I am denying the power of God to express through me. Speak as Jesus spoke, "I am light, I am love, I am a way shower, I am a peace keeper, I am an overcomer!"

These are the kinds of words that empower us to tune into the I Am that we already are!

Chapter Sixteen

Evil

Jesus never said: *"The Devil made me do it."*

"Fear is the tool of a man-made devil." ~ Napoleon Hill

The first Principle of the Unity Movement co-founded by Charles and Myrtle Fillmore teaches that, *"There is only one power in my life and in the universe...the all loving goodness of God!"* Mark 12:29 says that, *"the Lord is One"* and that means there is no other enduring power that can oppose this source of all life.

Consider this amazing verse from Ephesians:

"There is one body and one Spirit, just as you were called to the one hope of your calling, one Lord, one faith, one baptism, one God and Father of all, who is above all and through all and in all." ~ Ephesians 4:4-6

There is not another power in the Universe other than the One. There cannot be any power that opposes this one Spirit and everything exists within this loving energy that we call God.

There are many religions that embrace the idea of duality – that there is a negative entity called the Devil that steals souls from God and enjoys making people sin. He is very powerful and rules the current world we live in or so they say. Many people grow up with this kind of dualistic thinking and believe that everything is black and white. The truth is humans are inherently good but have the power of choice. This is what makes us complex and interesting. We are creative beings and we also have a shadow side. It is the dark parts of the human mind that create a chaotic world. Rather than taking responsibility for our actions and beliefs, we use the Devil, Satan, Lucifer, demons and other nefarious beings as scapegoats.

You will find these many terms in the Bible, which have confused many. They are labels that describe certain ideas that were understood differently in ancient times. They were not real entities, doing bad things to good people. They were actually psychological concepts used to describe deep inner processes. Books have been written and movies have been made to show them as real beings with very dark agendas. These energies get life from our negative thinking and become thought forms held together by our collective beliefs. If you believe in them you are giving your power away to something that reflects your shadow side. Many of the problems in the world stem from our spiritual immaturity and our lack of self-love.

A Fallen Star

Some claim the Devil is a fallen angel who is trying to take revenge against the Almighty for casting him out of heaven. ***Jesus never said*** anything about the Devil or Satan being a fallen angel, and the idea is not in the New Testament. In Isaiah, Chapter 4:12-16, these verses talk about Lucifer falling from heaven. It is actually speaking about the King of Babylon falling from heaven or his high political standing. The name Lucifer means *the morning star* and this King of Babylon became a Lucifer or star that fell from his exalted place among his people. Lucifer is not a real spiritual power but can be a person who comes from a place of pride, arrogance and narcissism.

Living In Ignorance

Evil spelled backwards is the word "live" and denotes the idea of *spiritual ignorance*. It is our lack of wisdom and information that blinds us. *Calamity* is another good definition of evil in Jesus' teachings too. Calamity is when something happens in our lives that we define as harmful to us. The word evil in those days had a different connotation than it does in modern times. Today we define evil as someone or something that is intrinsically bad instead of the ancient usage of *having a trouble or challenge that shows up unexpectedly in your life. Evil is the idea of harming one's self, or others, through willful ignorance.*

Why Do Bad Things Happen?

"These figs are very evil!" ~Jeremiah 24:8

How are figs evil? The word evil in this case means unripe or immature. Figs are not good or evil, they are just figs. People that are ignorant of universal truths may believe they are right in their beliefs in superiority. People get comfortable in constantly blaming another for their own ills. This is what kids do in high school in their lack of maturity. Many people act out their repressed anger and frustration by striking out against others and even killing them. This is the arrogant ignorance of *troubled and vengeful thinking.* If we really understood that every person is a child of God, then we would treat each other accordingly. Every person is sacred and holy. Superiority is a trick of the ego to make it feel better and is what causes most of the world's violence, torture and murder.

We live in a world where most people believe in duality, which means there is always a choice to make about how we respond to life's challenges. The words positive and negative are lesser "charged" words than good and evil and describe the mechanics of what is happening. There is always a balancing of the energy that is put out and we shall reap what we have sown. When we throw the boomerang of life out it always comes back to us, sometimes in unexpected ways. Collective belief systems are so ingrained in people that they sometimes reap the errors of their culture and family lineage. When a person grows up in a violent family or culture, they may believe that blaming and violence is the only way to behave. They end up putting that kind of energy out into the world. However, whatever we put out is what we will get back, until someone stops the destructive cycle, it will continue.

Darkness or unconsciousness in the mind cannot see the light until it receives some illumination. In reality the darkness actually teaches us to look for the light.

> *"This is the message we have heard from him and proclaim to you, that God is light and in him is no darkness at all." ~ 1 John 1:5*

Darkness is the inability to recognize and understand the truth. The light speaks of the higher intelligence and a clarity that exists when we align with it. Jesus said he was the light and he declared that we are the light, too. We are all children of the light and are here to show the way by walking in the light of our own true nature.

Satan

The name Satan denotes one who is an *accuser, blamer and troublemaker*. It is not a literal being with a pitchfork and horns, running around in a red underwear suit. There is no third party outside of us trying to make us sin. The trouble with Satan is that many people buy into the concept of an external entity that is constantly tempting us; Satan is always hanging around and bugging people. Once you let go of that belief and change your concept of what Satan is, you won't see him in your life anymore! This is the power of your mind, to believe and create your experience.

Growing up, I remember envisioning all kinds of weird phenomena, and ended up scaring myself to the point I had to keep the lights on at night into my early adulthood. Every time something happened that I perceived of as bad or negative I would blame it on Satan. Satan became a scapegoat for any number of things going wrong in my life. Once I took responsibility and reclaimed the power for my own life I was able to find some peace. The real Satan was negative programming from my own mind that was doing the blaming and accusing!

"Jesus turned to Peter and said, "Get behind me Satan!"
~ Matthew 16:23

When Jesus said these words he was speaking directly to Peter who happened to be disagreeing with him at the time. In that moment Peter was acting as an adversary against Jesus and his mission. He was repeating the thoughts from his own fearful thinking, but Jesus would have none of it. If Satan is actually just a voice in our head that is constantly criticizing us then we have the capacity to change our thoughts and change our circumstances. Jesus shows how we overcome by putting the condemning voice out of the mind so that it no longer affects us or cause us to feel bad. "Get behind me Satan," means just that. I put the blaming, accusing thoughts away and choose new and empowering thoughts to replace them. You cannot think two thoughts at once. Believe me I have tried. We can truly only focus on one thought at a time. If I am choosing a positive thought then there is no room for Satan or negative thinking.

Devil

The word Devil is a slang term for "doer of evil" and symbolizes a person who creates chaotic circumstances leading to calamity. It also means *divider* or any person that believes strongly in duality and the power of negativity. Unfortunately, there are a lot of religious leaders who fit this definition. They believe very strongly in duality and give great power to the negative aspects of life, this devilish concept is so strongly taught that it easily takes hold in people's minds. It can take some time to overcome this kind of belief system because it becomes ingrained in a person at an early age.

"A double minded man is unstable in all his ways."
~ James 1:8

How can we let go of this kind of idea?

We need to *cast out* the concept of a personal devil from our consciousness! That brings the responsibility back to us where it should be. Having a duality consciousness causes us to give away our power to something outside of ourselves. The Higher Power already dwells in every molecule of your body and you don't have to go anywhere in order to connect and find wholeness.

Do you know people with a "devil consciousness" that constantly create calamity in their own lives and others too? They get caught up in one negative experience and activity after another.

In ancient times, people understood these terms and knew what they meant. They understood the symbolism behind the words and the teachings. A "devil" is a person who has become mentally possessed by fearful thinking. Fear and anxiety tend to be their main expression of living and being in the world. These people are obsessed with the darkness (ignorance) of unconsciousness (unfocused attention). This fear-filled way of living is what creates one conflict after another. Fear is dread and it is poison to the body when it goes beyond the natural awareness of safety. Yes I want to look both ways before I cross the road and I don't want to drive without wearing a seat belt. That is my natural awareness of positive self-care. The problem comes when I begin to tell myself stories about how life should or shouldn't be. That is when I can easily become caught up in fear and become my own "devil", so to speak, and bring calamity upon myself.

Snakes and Dragons

"Now the serpent was craftier than any beast of the field, which the Lord God had made. And he said to the woman, "Indeed has God said, "You shall not eat from any tree of the garden?" ~ Genesis 3:1

The serpent and the dragon are some of the oldest symbols in the world. The serpent can symbolize the use of the brain in people with narcissistic tendencies. They desire to use others for their own purpose and self-interest. In the language of symbolism a serpent or snake can represent both positive and negative ideas and thoughts. It all depends on the way you perceive snakes. If you were taught to fear them as a child then most likely it will be a negative symbol in your dreams. On the other hand Native Americans saw snakes in a more positive light.

The dragon is a mythical creature that flies around breathing fire and destroying others. A dragon is symbolic of the collective thinking of the human mind that is in error and opposes right-minded thought. These are the beliefs and assumptions made in our society that are contrary to the sacredness of all life.

Lord Of The Flies

Beelzebub is another name that has been attributed to a being competing with the One God. Beelzebub is the "Lord of the flies" and was worshipped by the Philistines in an effort to try and control the population of flies and pesky insects. Beelzebub was also called the dung God. Gods were created by the people in ancient times to try and gain more control over the world around them. These terms were labels that gave the ancient people a way of communicating certain ideas. Not only did we create these so called enemies of God's goodness in the ancient world but also we are still doing it today!

The Walking Dead

Zombies seem to have made a comeback in our collective culture. These beings devoid of conscience and real awareness stumble and drag themselves around trying to find an energy source to feed upon. The zombie symbolizes a person who is not aware of his or her own inner light. If a Zombie bites you then you could become one too, especially if you allow them to infect you. It is important to keep our minds from being infected by the troubled thinking of others. Only unconditional love can heal a zombie. A zombie is simply a person who has lost touch with life and living and searches unconsciously for something to make them feel better.

That Draining Feeling

The *vampire* is also another metaphor for those who drain energy from us because they do not know how to care for themselves. People who talk too much do not realize the toll they take on another person's energy. Those who feel they are perpetual victims of life's circumstances also drain us of energy. People who do not practice self-care are always needy and never seem to have enough. Their unhealthy emotional state will create a constant pull on your energy if you allow it.

There are any number of popular movies and books that portray the sad existence of the living dead. It is because of widespread fear and loneliness that people lose their feeling sense of aliveness. An energy vampire must learn to be responsible for his or her own energy in order to be healed. All the monsters created by pop culture represent our fears that life is beyond our control. We may not be able to control everything in our lives but much of it can be managed in a positive way. Self-mastery is a higher way to use our power rightly by working to change ourselves. This is the kind of healing work Jesus did and that we can do too!

"Heal the sick, raise the dead, cleanse the lepers, and cast out demons. You received without paying; give without pay." ~ Matthew 10:8

This scripture has been taken literally by many but when is the last time you have saw the dead raised up? Can you imagine Uncle Fred rising up out of the coffin after a fervent prayer? While any of these feats may be possible, the point Jesus is really making, especially since he *only* spoke in *parables* and *metaphors* is that we have the power within us to do great things!

Heal The Sick

Many times physical sickness is brought about through our ignorance of what it truly means to be well and whole. Sickness does not happen to us because we are bad people in need of punishment. It's what we don't know about ourselves and how our body-mind connection actually works. Real healing takes place within us first and then can manifest in the physical body. Jesus healed the sense of separation that people felt between themselves and God. Many of them also found physical healing too. We can all be healing agents who can assist others in their recovery from the programmed patterns of negative thinking and the unconscious lifestyle.

Albert Einstein said, "Everything is energy." Energy is the blueprint for our physical bodies. Even before someone discovers they have a physical illness the energy body is already holding the negative pattern. We must keep our energy clear if we want to be healthy. When Jesus touched people he was correcting their energy so they could become well. Love and compassion is the motivation behind all healing. Jesus demonstrated that love and compassion could heal a multitude of errors and inner wounds.

Raise The Dead

Raising the dead is awakening someone who is unconscious or asleep to their divine potential. Many people have lost touch with their inner spirit and do not have the warmth associated with someone in touch with their spiritual essence. You raise the dead by raising the consciousness of people. It's part of our calling as spiritual practitioners of grace and peace to share the unconditional love we have actualized in ourselves.

Have you helped to heal a zombie today?

Cleanse The Leper

The physical lepers of ancient times were outcasts and considered unclean and untouchable. They would travel together and lived outside of the cities, away from their families and the people they loved. Today we have societal lepers who have been isolated by our culture because they do not fit our "normal" stereotype. Many gender, racial, and sexual biases exist in our culture today. People who are prejudiced and judgmental see "others" as unclean and untouchable. We must heal the lepers of today who feel separated from the mainstream, and make them feel welcome. There is a great need of inner healing for all who are wounded because they are deemed different.

We are all children of God and that is what binds us together. Love and forgiveness can heal a multitude of wounds. Now is the time to begin the healing work of cleansing the lepers, by healing our own perception first. We are all God's children, and we have a right to be whatever the Creator has made each of us to be. Leprosy is a symbolic sense of unworthiness and low self esteem, and much of it comes from religious condemnation and guilt.

Cast Out Demons

Do you feel like you're being chased by evil spirits who want to do you harm? An evil spirit represents an overstressed individual that uses their energy to create negative thought forms and patterns.

Consider how Jesus metaphorically describes this process:

> *"When the unclean spirit has gone out of a person, it wanders through waterless regions looking for a resting place, but it finds none.*
>
> *Then it says, 'I will return to my house from which I came.' When it comes, it finds it empty, swept, and put in order.*
>
> *Then it goes and brings along seven other spirits more evil than itself, and they enter and live there; and the last state of that person is worse than the first.*
> *~ Matthew 12:43-45*

The mind can create sub-personalities, which can be angry and potentially violent. Sometimes we hear a voice in our head that is obsessively negative and self-defeating. This part of our self can be dealt with by renewing the mind, and releasing the negative energies created through our misperceptions. These sub-personalities, which blame and accuse us, need to be released and re-absorbed back into the field of our vital energy. It is important to take responsibility for our thoughts and feelings. Once we own them, we can change and transform them into useful fuel for our lives.

The above words of Jesus reveal how our negative patterned thinking that is swept out will ultimately come back if we do not fill our minds with positive thoughts and feelings. These sub-personalities (beliefs and attitudes) do not have to torture us, unless we continue to entertain them and allow them to set up residence in our minds. For example, many people who have addictions exhibit a totally different personality that takes over when they are under the influence, or when they are desperately trying to get a fix.

As we have discussed, the real Satan or Devil is the one inside your head that blames and accuses you and could be called the negative ego. We also have a positive ego that becomes the servant of Spirit by yielding to the higher mind. As long as you are alive you will have an ego, so it's important that you use yours in the proper context.

False Prophets

"Beware of false prophets who come disguised as harmless sheep but are inwardly ravenous wolves."
~ Matthew 7:15

Be aware of predators who seek to devour the life force of others. Sociopaths are predators who have little or no conscience or sense of empathy. They are children of God too, but they are also predators, just like tigers in the wild are. Many of them become our politicians, CEOs of corporations, ministers, doctors, and lawyers... and could be involved in leadership positions of all kinds. They seek the public eye and enjoy lording over others to get their own way. They have a strong drive to succeed and will use any means necessary to do so. They only show an interest in you if you have something they want or can use.

It is my opinion that many of our politicians today exhibit sociopathic behavior. They can say almost anything to get elected and then use their office to further their career rather than representing the people who elected them. They have no idea about the concept of the "highest good for all" or what it truly means to "be your brother or sister's keeper." It is amazing how "we the people" can keep electing leaders that have no demonstrable sense of compassion!

Modern brain scans can reveal the missing part of the brain that controls empathy and science is beginning to confirm this. A recent article claimed that one out of every hundred people do not have the ability to empathize or feel the pain of others. It is important to be aware of these individuals. They are a part of the societal landscape Jesus warned us about. Not that we should fear them but that we can have a watchful eye out so we will not be used by them. We need to be able to look at the fruit of the tree and discern what the root is. The root determines the fruit. People who are sociopaths are cold inside but sometimes can put on a false front, appearing warm and charismatic. Just having an awareness of these kinds of people will help you to avoid much trouble.

This is not about judging anyone. It is the same idea that I need to be cautious around lions, tigers and bears. Because they are predators I might be mistaken for lunch...

Discerning Intents And Attitudes

False prophets and self-centered gurus also need to be recognized. Some people invest their entire life savings in spiritual scams that leave them cold and indifferent. We must use spiritual discernment and avoid the snakes in the grass. The more light you experience and wisdom you gain, the more you will be able to clearly see those who do not have your best interests in mind. Test the spirit of intent and see if compassion and true integrity are at the core of any teaching you listen to. It is not necessary to judge the person, but to look at their fruits and see if what they offer is spiritually beneficial!

Sometimes those with great light also have the greatest unhealed shadow. We want to choose our spiritual path wisely. We can waste a lot of years on a path that is not a fit for us. Many times this will appeal to our sense of entitlement and desire for a shortcut to enlightenment and there we go, off to the races.

"Dear friends, do not believe every spirit, but test the spirits to see whether they are from God, because many false prophets have gone out into the world." ~ 1 John 4:1

Questioning is Allowed

The word used *to test or discern* in the Bible speaks of *seeing into the truth of a person or a thing*. Any spiritual teacher who does not allow questioning may be hiding something from you. Any person claiming enlightenment and also wants lots of your money is a likely suspect too. Don't be a sheep that simply follows the loudest voice in the fold. Just because a person can speak all the latest spiritual buzzwords does not mean they are enlightened.

We live at a time where we can Google people and see what others are saying about them. While it's true you can't believe all the bad press that someone receives on the Internet, it's just as true that if there are many former followers that claim abuse or have been harmed in some way, then you should probably heed what is being said. This is especially true if former followers have begun a recovery program to overcome the brainwashing and damage done to them.

Don't throw your life away on something that has an appearance of spirituality but lacks the true power of love as its motivation! Look within and experience your own divinity. Be your own Guru! In the final analysis, you are responsible for your own soul and the path you take.

Just because a lot of people believe something does not make it true. Most human thought simply transfers from one person and generation to another unquestioned, and much of it is negatively oriented. As eternal souls we've been on this journey for a long while and it's always good "to test the spirits," – the root attitudes and intentions – to determine if a spiritual path is truly worthy of your time and trust.

Never be afraid to question and investigate any and every spiritual program. Your soul is most precious and you never want to hand it over to a narcissistic group or individual who only wants to use you. Allow your spiritual awareness to be your guide.

If you stay with the One Power that will never leave you or lead you astray, you will be just fine. By having a belief in "The One Power and The One Presence" you release all the other so called gods, demons and darkness, which are nothing more than unhealed energies of the unconscious mind.

Chapter Seventeen

The Word

***Jesus never said:** "Only use the King James version because in it God has personally written down everything he ever said and nothing else can ever be added."*

"In the beginning was the Word, and the Word was with God, and the Word was God. He was in the beginning with God. All things were made through him, and without him was not anything made that was made."
~ John 1:1-3

There are a lot of quotes **Jesus did not say** that many people attribute to him. So how can we know what's really the inspired writings of sacred scripture? What is the word of God and how do we know if we have it? Did God actually speak to humanity in the first place? Is the living word still expressing itself today? These are some of the questions that need to be explored.

What is commonly called the teachings of Jesus reveal wonderful truths, which can be helpful to us on our spiritual path. Millions of people have discovered these universal principles and they have changed their lives for the better. The sayings of Jesus are very positive, and when applied to our personal lives, lead us to be better citizens of the world. The challenge is to know which of the sayings were actually given without editing or translation

137

errors. At this time there is no way to know for certain if some early scholars added a word or sentence here or there in order to influence people with their particular belief system.

Much of the New Testament was written 60 to 100 years after Jesus. The writers had to rely on those who knew somebody that knew the disciples on a personal basis, and then passed on their ideas about what Jesus said. There were several documents at the time claiming genuine authenticity in the writings. You couldn't check out the sayings of Jesus from the local library, bookstore, or his personal blog! There were actually many books about Jesus and the gospel, which were held by individuals claiming to have the true, inspired words that Jesus spoke.

What constitutes the Word of God? Once you have a definition that works then you can read nearly any so called scriptural writing and discern the truth for yourself.

"For the word of God is alive and powerful. It is sharper than the sharpest two-edged sword, cutting between soul and spirit, between joint and marrow. It exposes our innermost thoughts and desires." ~ Hebrews 4:12

There is true power and aliveness in the words that come from God. The word of God is not rote language, which is dull, containing no life. Rather, it slices through the false persona and points to the truth. It manifests in us, revealing the inner world of intuition and genuine confidence. It is the essence of the knowing part of your being that already resonates as the true word of God.

"In the Greek language, one of the words for "word" is Logos. It originates from classical Greek thought, which refers to a universal divine reason, immanent in nature,

yet transcending all oppositions and imperfections in the cosmos and humanity. An eternal and unchanging truth present from the time of creation, available to every individual who seeks it. A unifying and liberating revelatory force which connects the human with the divine; manifested in the world as an act of God's love in the form of the Christ." ~ Wikipedia

The word of God is alive and powerful, and comes from a spiritual place within the heart. The word of God still arises today from anyone who is in touch with his or her own true, authentic spirit. God spoke to people of the ancient world at the level they could receive it and still speaks to us today. Holy Spirit continues to reveal the truth to all who are open and prepared to listen.

Love's Motivation

Love is the very foundation of any and all true spiritual teachings. The word *God* is actually another word for *Love*. How does that resonate with you? Can you trust your own intuition? Love is the answer and love is the way. If love is not important in a spiritual teaching, then it is not something that will work for me. How about you?

We have the right to determine our beliefs and if they really work. The Divine Mind only operates through love and universal truth. If it is true for one then it must be true for all. If a spiritual tradition does not include kindness and mercy, can you truly endorse it? Can there truly be heaven on earth without the enlightened application of love, kindness and mercy?

Does It Inspire And Is It Practical?

Words that lead to a life better lived are words to hear and apply. Sayings which instruct how to be the best version of yourself are inspired words. Words that have no effect are usually ideas or thoughts from the ego. Practicality is the simple elegant quality of truth. A genuine word from God must be inspiring and practical.

It has to be practical and it needs to work for you and me. Jesus said, "You will know a person by the fruit they bear." Real truth can be applied by anyone and the results will follow. We live in the day of great promises and little delivery. If I am going to invest my life in any teaching or philosophy then I want it to work. Not only must it be practical but also it is universal and does not apply only to a chosen few.

The *Logos (word from God)* refers to the divine logic that is higher than our small ego minds. Many people look at the world and cannot see the divine logic that orders and arranges the cosmos. This greater Intelligence exists within each and every one of us. We all have The Logos as our guide but not all understand it. There really is a higher order to our lives that makes perfect sense on an inner level.

The "little mind" judges only by the outward appearance. The living word of God is ever available to us right now. It comes to us through original ideas and inspired thinking that happens when we live in faith coupled with a creative imagination. All the great thinkers delved deeply into themselves to pull out the logos of wisdom and knowledge. This is where all our great inventions come from too. Language and math began from this inner knowing place. Anything that works well and moves us forward in life comes from this higher logic.

Whenever you read something that is supposed to be inspired, there are some guidelines to determine if it is a positive truth that will assist you on your spiritual path:
Does it adhere to The Golden Rule? "Do to others what you will have them do to you" is inspired and feels right. Every major religion has its own version of The Golden Rule. It's a universal truth relevant to whatever age we live in and will always do us good.

Does it manipulate? Inspired teachings do not manipulate people through fear and guilt.

What Is Truth?

Webster's dictionary defines truth as, "The state of being the case, fact, the body of real things, events, actuality." Outer truth is based on what is real and factual. It is different from spiritual truth, which is dependent upon the level of awareness one has attained. Infinite Intelligence cannot be perceived and understood in its entirety all at once. A revelation usually unfolds gradually inside a person's heart and mind. God is realized and uncovered in steps and stages. The truth is always the same, but our perception grows and changes so we can adapt as we go along. One New Testament writer states:

"Therefore let us move beyond the elementary teachings about Christ and be taken forward to maturity."
~ Hebrews 6:1

I have three sons who are all at different states of awareness about life and the world. They each have their own perspective and sometimes they have agreed with me and sometimes they have not...Surprise! They all have the right to believe what they want and arrive at conclusions according to their own understanding. When my oldest son was a child I couldn't wait for him to grow up so I could share with him on an equal basis. As a small child he believed in Santa Claus and the Easter bunny. That doesn't mean he was ignorant, but merely that he was a child and that is what he and many other children believe.

The day came when he could make up his own mind about the truths of life. We still talk sometimes, and I honor his beliefs and ideas. Even though we are related, his experience of life is different than mine. Therefore, he may have come to different conclusions than I have. That is just fine with me because he is an independent thinker. I never wanted carbon copies of myself in my children (well, maybe at first I did), though now, I realize the value of allowing them to be their own person and learn for themselves. Their truth is born from their own experience and desire for growth.

"Be established in the present truth." ~ 2 Peter 1:12

Real truth is not handed down from the past, it is realized and discovered for oneself in each now moment. Most of us have struggled with knowing the "ultimate truth", which is beyond most of our ability to grasp.

Many of us are still in the childhood stages of understanding and awareness, and do not comprehend the idea of infinity, which seemingly contradicts our linear thinking. Truth is not an intellectual pursuit; it is spiritually intuited and perceived. It is an inner change and transformation, like the early morning light that grows (It "dawns on us") until the full sunshine of knowledge bathes us in the warm, full strength of Truth.

The word of God is both an individual and collective revelation. Intuitive people receive it and then teach it to the world. The only problem is that as soon as it is taught it becomes second hand knowledge. Direct revelation can be confirmed through our life's journey as we prove it to ourselves. The old saying goes, "If you give a man a fish you feed him for a day. Teach him how to fish and he will be fed for a lifetime." We must, ultimately, learn to prove the Truth for ourselves! Unless it works for you it is just intellectual, unformed musings. These musings are fine and good, but until they are proven in the laboratory of your life, you still don't have the Truth. Be wary of people who claim ultimate truth; usually, they want to sell it to you.

I used to buy into everything that came down the pike, but today I am more selective and discerning. I remain open-minded and understand that there is still a need to grow. In this life, we will probably never understand it all. We are here to receive what we need when we need it.

Similarly, some teachers claim to be enlightened, which can sound very appealing. As you investigate different spiritual concepts, ideas and philosophies on your spiritual quest for the Truth, you will learn from most of them. A few you will see through right away because of your experiences and background of self-study and spiritual education. You will discover fairly quickly that no one school of religious studies can give you all the truth you need. There is almost always some kind of bias involved in most belief systems. When you can be okay with this, you take what works and leave the rest.

So how do you know the word of God for yourself? You have to discern the truth through trial and error and then allow it to form itself inside of you. You must be responsible. Never give up your right to decide your Truth to anyone else. If you discover various authors and teachers that resonate with you, and you trust what they have to say, align yourself with those who you intuit to be on the same path. Do not be a self-absorbed lone ranger on your spiritual journey.

When you read the Bible or any other writing, use your inner gauge to guide you and help you see the Truth. When you see the truth it makes an immediate impact on your life right now, while at the same time it is ever evolving and growing, and you change.

Are We Free Yet?

In summary, spiritual truth must be practical, universal and based solidly in love. It should be relevant to your life, and not some airy-fairy, pie-in-the-sky, far off idea with no practical value. It must work for you in life here and now. It should be confirmed through other spiritual teachings and not be ego driven. It must also inspire you to rise higher and live better. It will always guide you to be a compassionate person who cares for all people in your sphere of influence. If it is alive and powerful, then you will receive it into your heart and mind and you will be changed for the better!

And finally, it must bring about peace, and a feeling of inner freedom.

After all, Jesus did say, *"The truth will make you free."*

Chapter Eighteen

Prayer

Jesus never said: *"Keep begging for what you want and it just might work."*

The function of prayer is not to influence God, but rather to change the nature of the one who prays."
~ Soren Kierkegaard

Jesus was sharing powerful universal truths about a God that is Spirit rather than a physical being with arms and legs. He was relating ideas on how to interact with this Divine Power in a positive way. Many people still see God as the image of a human being with supernatural abilities. It's as if God is this old man sitting on the clouds in the sky looking down on us all and judging everyone. If he is in a good mood he might have pity on us and answer our pleadings for help, but only if we are good enough. Many people view God as a stern parental figure who may or may not answer their prayers.

If you understand that God is Spirit and present everywhere, it makes greater sense and infinitely expands your prayer potential. Having two arms and two legs is really a limitation because you can only be in one place at a time.

Jesus said,

"Don't you know that you are gods?"
~ John 10:34

It may be hard for you to contemplate the idea of being a god, but that is what Jesus said. There are several different words for God or Lord in the Bible and each one reveals a unique aspect of the divine nature. In this particular verse, the word god is *Elohim,* which means *creators.* Jesus was saying that we are all divine beings with creative ability. We are the creators of our reality! This is very good news because it means we have the power to create our world and make it the way we want it to be. If there is something you do not like about your experience why not take personal responsibility for it and make some changes?

So Then How Shall We Pray?

Jesus actually answers this question directly in the Gospels. This is the famous prayer repeated in a variety of Christian denominations around the world. Jesus said to pray in this manner; he did not necessarily say to pray with the exact wording he used. This prayer is a practical outline we can use to pray most effectively, although I believe any prayer that works for you is a good thing. There are some deep truths hidden in the Lord's Prayer and it holds a special key, but only when we know and understand that God is Spirit. This is the only way all of our prayers could actually have meaning and receive answers to them.

Holy Spirit - Holy Energy

Another way to describe spirit is as energy. Einstein taught us that, "Everything in the universe is made of energy." The Scripture says that Spirit made all things. Spirit is an old fashioned term for what today we would call energy. This

146

spiritual energy is the creative substance and raw material of life itself. Everything that exists is imbued with this Holy Spiritual Energy. This power is the life force that fills all things.

The disciples asked Jesus, "How then shall we pray?"

That's when Jesus modeled a perfect prayer with many truths hidden in every word. This prayer came to be known as the Lord's Prayer, and has been repeatedly spoken for nearly 2000 years. There are different levels of understanding about how these prayer secrets can assist us in having a positive effect in our lives.

The Lord's Prayer is not a form of begging or beseeching, addressed to a nebulous God "out there" somewhere. It is a powerful, yet simple, affirmative prayer, in perfect alignment with universal principle about the nature of divinity. It includes how we can truly relate to that powerful spiritual energy and how we can see our true desires manifest.

"Our Father, which art in heaven"

We are in relationship with this sacred energy like that of a parent, but without the dysfunction. It speaks of the closeness between a child and its attentive and loving parent. God is not far off and we don't have to be afraid, because this power of God is within us. The connection is already there and as a child of God we have a right to access this inner power. *Abba* is the Greek word for *Father* and literally means *Papa*, which is a tender word denoting a loving relationship. We begin our prayer to our Father, our loving source of all that we need, our Papa. We say *Our* Father which is different than addressing *my or your* Father.

Jesus used the word "our" so we understand that God is every person's spiritual parent! It is through love that prayer is made in and through us, like a small child asking his or her Father or Mother for something to eat. There is no hesitation in the child because it feels the connection with the Parents; Dad and Mom will not fail to provide for their beloved child.

We connect through this loving vibrational feeling that resonates, with who we are and what potential we have.

This is how we access the holy spiritual energy of life itself in a loving and creative way. Take a moment to breathe deeply and sense this pure creative energy that is in you now.

"Hallowed be thy name"

The name of God is love and it is sacred inside of our being. Within us is the "secret place of the Most high". Jesus said to go inside your "secret closet" and discover your connection with this sacred presence. It's important to find that awe inspired feeling as we recognize the nature of our true being. Hold that sacred feeling in your heart as you pray and affirm the good that is already yours. In this space, allow a divine idea to come into your consciousness. Be open to receiving a new thought, or even feeling a sense of the sacred. All of this is evidence of your sweet connection with Divinity.

"Thy kingdom come"

This inner Kingdom will bear fruit within us as we meditate and contemplate its essence. It is the sense of giving birth to a divine idea that is ready to be born. As you hold a desire in your being it begins to grow inside you, like a baby being formed in its mother's womb. We nurture this infant awareness and continue to let it incubate in our hearts. Feel this idea growing within you now. The kingdom is coming to express itself in and through your life.

"Thy will be done in earth as it is in heaven."

It is now time to speak words from the same feeling and belief you have inside and begin to affirm that, yes, you are pregnant with a divine idea and the child is about to be born. Agree with your heart's desire and know beyond any doubt that it is coming from the heaven inside you into the physical world of manifestation. See it coming forth in your mind's eye and it will not fail to appear.

"Give us this day our daily bread"

Now receive the bread of understanding and feed on it so that the way is made clear. Choose, daily, to affirm this idea and feed on the goodness of its vibrational energy. Each day the idea grows, as Jesus said, "I have food to eat of that you know nothing about." People around you may not see what you see and cannot understand your passion until the idea is made manifest. Enjoy each day for what it

149

brings forth and know that each day leads to the fulfillment of your prayers.

"And forgive us our debts, as we also have forgiven our debtors"

We must remember to forgive others for not understanding our mission and purpose. Our good can only be blocked when we refuse to release and forgive others. We will hold ourselves in bondage until we can let go and release the captives from the prison of our own mind. The idea of forgiveness from the New Testament is about complete detachment from someone or something. It is like a branch that has fallen from a tree and is no longer a part of the tree and withers away. When you no longer feed on negative thinking about a person or situation then the branch of unforgiveness and resentment will fall off your tree and die. It can no longer interfere with your prayers. Forgiveness is a powerful way to release your self and become free. Do it now and do it often...

"And leave us not in temptation, but deliver us from evil."

Jesus told us in another place that God does not tempt us and therefore Spirit does not guide us toward failure and trouble. That is what we do to ourselves. So the best approach to this verse is the idea that God will not *leave us* in temptation but will guide us through it! The word evil in this sense speaks of calamity and trouble. May we all make our way through the negativity of our own minds and be delivered into the light of a new day.

"For yours is the kingdom and the power and the glory forever."

Give thanks and proclaim your gratitude for the perfect aligning with the true God of your being. Connect forever and delight in this Kingdom of power continually.

Despite only lightly touching on the metaphysical depths suggested by this familiar, and deceptively simple, prayer, enough guidance is revealed for you to begin manifesting whatever your heaven or bliss is into this earth! Begin now and your awareness and understanding will continue to grow.

By adapting your attitudes and tuning them to a higher vibration, you can learn to live in a continuous state of good fortune and blessing.

Chapter Nineteen

Attitudes

Jesus never said: *"Blessed are the religious do-gooders for they shall be my favorites."*

"A bad habit is like a flat tire, if you don't change it you will never go anywhere." ~ Inspirationboost.com

"We can complain because rosebushes have thorns, or rejoice because thorn bushes have roses."
~ Abraham Lincoln

Jesus stood on a lovely hillside by the water and shared the positive attitudes of a happy and blessed life. These attitudes make a wonderful doctrinal statement for any spiritual community that follows Jesus' gospel of divine ideas. This is the main thrust of Jesus' teachings. They actually have the power to transform the world's consciousness into something deeply fulfilling. These truths are very practical, and when applied, they are guaranteed to make a difference in your life.

The word beatitude comes from the Latin *beatus,* which means to make happy, and it implies good fortune. The eight Beatitudes are life-affirming attitudes that lead to true happiness. These eight keys of happiness reveal the high quality of life that Jesus not only talked about, but also demonstrated. They are part of the inner laws of a new Heaven (consciousness) and new Earth (ways of living). These Beatitudes lead to an enlightened state of being and greater spiritual awareness, and are proof that God wants YOU and me to be happy and blessed.

You will be blessed, fortunate and happy when you live your life based on these beautiful attitudes.

Jesus came to share with all who would listen, and to those that realized they needed to change. He spoke to average people that consisted of farmers, fishermen and laborers... those who might be called the "religious outcasts" of that day. The Pharisees and Sadducees were the religious elite – the religious Jews, who followed a caste system of that time and were not interested in change.

These beautiful attitudes were more than just religious rules about keeping your hands washed or taking a day off from work one day a week. They have the power to transform your life through simple application. Unfortunately only the wealthy of that time could manage to keep up with all the commandments of the law. The common laborers of the day were busy working and taking care of their families. They did not have enough time to practice the law, so they would have to regularly bring an animal to sacrifice for their "sins". Jesus wanted to show them the true and more natural state of life, so they could experience their divine potential.

The Beatitudes are found in Matthew 5:1-12... I will quote the Beatitude and then give you my understanding of what it means in italics.

"Blessed are the poor in spirit, for theirs is the kingdom of heaven."

Happy And Fortunate Are Those Who Empty Themselves Of False Personae For They Will Uncover Their Inner Bliss.

Jesus was telling them how fortunate they really were, because, in spite of all the binding laws of the time, they could discover a peaceful way of life that was free from religious duties. His teaching empowered them to take responsibility for their own lives. They were not born to be second-class citizens as taught by the priests. They were all children of God and if they would become "poor of spirit" or empty themselves of false self-beliefs and make their own connection with the higher power they could find real inner happiness.

When you act on the teachings of Jesus you will discover the kingdom of heaven, which is inside of you. Some people still mistakenly think Jesus meant "it is a virtue to be poor, and if you suffer patiently through your poverty, you'll have a reward in heaven."

Instead, blessed are you who are free from the man-made beliefs of culture, family and religion. You become open and receptive to the Truth, which comes from the spirit within. Education is important and necessary, but education alone cannot give you peace of mind. It's time for our modern world to find balance by listening more to the heart rather than just the intellect. We must empty out our false notions of unworthiness and lack. What does your heart tell you to do? Are you listening to the inner voice of spirit that wants to lead you to a prosperous and happy place? The truth is in you as this beatitude reveals. Trust the truth inside your being, which is where God has been all along.

Being poor means your intellect is not running the show and you are following the intuitive guidance of your heart.

New thought teacher Eric Butterworth says that the root word, which is translated "spirit" in this verse, is more accurately translated as "pride"...poor in pride, meaning to empty yourself and realize you cannot reach an understanding of God through the intellect alone. You must be as a little child and be teachable.

This beatitude is contrary to the ego, which already thinks it knows the truth. That is why we must empty ourselves of our false pride and religious personae.

The word "heaven" comes from a Hebrew root that means, "to expand and heave upward". It's the idea of raising our consciousness to a higher state where life becomes a blessing to us rather than a hardship. This kind of attitude means you are teachable and flexible. True lasting happiness comes to those that are open to new and different ways to live in the world.

How open is your mind? How attached are you to your opinions? These are the kinds of questions we must ask ourselves and then be accountable. This is a truly blessed and receptive state to be in. Once you empty yourself of what is blocking your good then God can fill you with all good things. The kingdom of peace, joy, love and laughter are naturally drawn to you when you have room for it!

"Blessed are the meek: for they shall inherit the earth."

Happy And Fortunate Are The One's Who Manage Their Inner Power – All The Blessings Of Earth Belong To Them.

So, are we supposed to just be doormats for people by letting them walk all over us so that one day we will become the rulers of the earth?

That doesn't make much sense.

Meekness does not mean weakness. Rather, Jesus is referring to an attitude toward God. Jesus said, "I, of myself, can do nothing." He recognized that the power came THROUGH him, not FROM him, and as long as he was in harmony with divinity, he could do great things.
Meekness is *natural gentleness* or the idea of *controlled strength*. True meekness is when great power is at your command and you have the ability to use it in a positive way. We must learn to marshal our forces and talents for good and apply them by using a light touch. A true craftsman does not destroy his tools by overly exerting force but by knowing when and how to use them most efficiently.

By activating our receptive mind we can then invite Divine Ideas to enter our thoughts. We don't want to be too impetuous to wait for the right moment or take time to listen for inspiration and guidance. True meekness is wisdom in action. Think about Gandhi and how he was able to change the state of an entire nation through humility and non-violent action. That is what Jesus was talking about.

Metaphysically speaking, the earth represents the consciousness of the physical body. When we work diligently, with awareness, to embrace this consciousness of meekness we can harness our inner potential, which allows us to become masters of our mind and body.

True control has nothing to do with an outward show of force, but is a gentle person, tuned in to creative ideas. The earth dimension becomes yours to enjoy when you are in touch with your inner strength.

> **"Blessed are they that hunger and thirst for righteousness for they shall be filled."**

Happy And Fortunate Are Those Who Are Passionate About Life – They Can Have It All.

Let us affirm together:

I now align my spirit, mind and body.

I use my mind for right thinking and positive thoughts.

I am in harmony with God and all that is sacred and holy.

Is it possible you may have an anger problem? Are you mad at God? Many people are and don't even know it! It's a deep-seated belief that God is picking on you for some obscure reason. I invite you to forgive God, not because the Divine Power has done anything to you, but because of a misconception about who and what Divinity really is. The true Lord of your being is always on your side and is working with you and for you.

Here are three valuable ways to satisfy your hunger and thirst and thus be filled with what you need.

- *Align with the Divine by forgiving God*
- *Align with your being by forgiving yourself*
- *Align with life by saying yes to life*

Righteousness comes through saying *yes* to life... and that means *no* to whatever is not life! I am a child of God. I am God's idea and God has only good ideas. To hunger and thirst is to have passion and when you hunger and thirst for God the same way you desire food and water you will be filled. If you hunger and thirst for right-mindedness you will make a difference in the world and help others find fulfillment too. What are you truly hungry and thirsty for? What do you really feel passionate about? This attitude will bring you what you need.

"Blessed are the merciful for they shall be shown mercy."

Happy And Fortunate Are The Compassionate – They Will Receive In The Same Manner As They Have Given.

Many in the world are experiencing a flowering of consciousness. At the same time, there are those who resist this new paradigm unfolding. We need to create more beauty in the world by showing mercy and radiating compassion toward others. The truly merciful possess an inner storehouse of good thoughts and feelings that gives them the confidence to share their gifts with the world. You must first have something to give before you can give it. You are the habitation of divinity and have much to share. This is a beautiful attitude to develop within your self.

You must believe in yourself and know that who you are is valuable. Your self-worth must be high enough to believe you have something worthy to give to others. Feeling sorry for others is just the ego endeavoring to be superior by saying, "I pity those poor souls who are not as good as me." Everyone on this planet has value and worth. Just because we are in a position of being able to give does not mean we are better than those we give to. All of us are children of

God, and when I have two coats I can share the extra coat with someone who has none. Does that mean I should only have one coat? The truth is I have many "coats" in my closet and I am blessed. Most of the people reading this are likely experiencing the same blessing.
Having many coats is not wrong. The error comes when you still feel lack and are unappreciative even when you have everything you need.

People say, "When I win the lottery, then I will be able to give to others." But that's not the point of this beatitude. Giving starts now. You can give of your time, talent and treasure for the good of humanity. Waiting until you are financially wealthy and have your act totally together before you start giving stops the flow of good in and through you in the now.

Giving is really about sharing yourself with others. I don't give just to feel good, although I do feel good when I give. I give because it is my true nature to do so. A flower gives you its color and its fragrance, not because it likes you, or because you deserve it. It gives freely to everyone, because that is its nature. The flower gives so that it may live.

I am merciful because it is the natural way of life. Use your talents and gifts to contribute to the circulation of life's blessings, starting now, however you can. Don't let fear keep you from expressing your true potential for compassion and sharing. When you use your gifts, you are centered in your oneness with divinity. You are doing what you came to this Earth to do and you are happy and fulfilled.

If you are a poet, write poetry and inspire others with it. If you sing, then sing as often as you can, just for the joy of singing. If you are an entrepreneur, then build your business and create value, prosperity and jobs for others along the way. Whatever your gift is, just share whatever you have to give. That is showing mercy and compassion. It's not just about giving to the poor and the needy, although that is important as well. It's about expressing your God given gift in this life right now! Until we do we are stuck in our own mental patterns of lack and limitation.

There Is Plenty For Everyone

It is our spiritual immaturity, our lack of love, compassion and mercy, which creates roadblocks to getting what is needed to everyone in the world. Many in power want to hoard it all for themselves because of greed, which is fear of lack. Down through the centuries England has had a few Kings and Queens who have ruled with the highest good in mind, and also some who have dominated and beaten their people into submission. We need those in authority that have an abundance consciousness – so that all people have access to what they need.

Without Compassion There Is No Circulation Of Good.

Have you noticed that it all gets back to love and kindness? Have a passion to joyously share your truth with others and you will be blessed. As you share your truth, it will cause others to think for them selves. Whether they agree or not, it gets a conversation started. If you hoard your time, talent and treasure then lack will appear, and you will never seem to get enough to be fulfilled. The energies of life must flow through you in order for you to find fulfillment and happiness. If you are living without compassion, then you will be sad and void of the life force, which needs a channel to flow through. Be that channel for the source of happiness and the supplier of good things.

The universal river of life makes its way through you and touches everyone around you. This river will energize you and you will be filled with enthusiasm and joy. It is a pleasure to give and it does make a difference. Giving has a definite feeling of rightness to it that you cannot deny.
Keep the circulation of good going and you will be surprised at what you can accomplish! You will find the happiness that you seek. Commit to letting your compassion flow, starting right here, right now, starting at the level of giving that's right for you. Don't wait!

"Blessed are they that mourn for they shall be comforted."

Happy And Fortunate Are Those Who Can Release Grief Through Expressing It – They Will Find Peace And Comfort.

Was Jesus saying that the more suffering you experience the better? Does suffering lead to heaven within? Not necessarily. The idea is to use your sorrow to find heaven within you and live a happy and prosperous life here and now. Joy is your natural state of being. You may be hurting, but you can overcome your challenges and change your life. Crying and tears can be a healing release of what is blocking this heaven within you. Mourning, or grieving, is not complaining. It is the inner activity of letting go of a loss.

If you obsess over losing something or someone, you can become emotionally stuck, and that keeps you from finding happiness and purpose. Using your losses to learn and grow, however, is optimal living at its best. Yes, of course we will grieve, and grieve we must, but we cannot stay in grief. This world is temporary, made up of many gains and losses.

Reverend Robert Schuller tells us, "Some people may ask why bad things happen to good people? The better question is: What happens to good people when bad things happen to them? What do good people do when the bad things happen?"

God wants to comfort you from within, but you need to make room by letting go of whatever needs to leave your life. When you ask why something happens the answer comes back immediately. The answer is always the "is-ness" of the situation. Whatever is happening is what is going on, so it's important to acknowledge it.

Do not resist. Recognize that this experience is here in your life right now. Acceptance is the quickest way to make peace with something, recognizing it as a momentary experience and knowing that it could shift at any time. In reality, it must shift as your awareness and thinking about it shifts. Receive the comfort of God's love, and know that whatever you face in your life is not forever. Look for the gift. Look for the lesson. What is this experience trying to tell you? We can become better or we can become bitter – it is always a choice. Find relief from grief by surrendering everything to God in the moment. This is how we can turn our mourning into something positive.

"Weeping only lasts through the night but joy comes in the morning." ~ King David

David said God would turn your mourning into joy. This is a wonderful promise if we will simply trust and focus on what is real and turn away from what is not. What can you do about your situation? What can God do for you, in you or through you about your situation?

The Divine gives us a courageous heart that is brave and willing to face our fears. You discover peace by quietly reflecting on the sweet presence of Spirit in the now moment. You have everything you need to live fully and be truly successful.

It is important that the idea of loss not run our lives. We want to look at the blessings already evident. Don't allow the past to control your present or your future. Make time daily to allow the comforting Presence of Spirit to be with you right in the midst of your situation, and you will return to a settled state of mind. Your mourning will be turned into joy, because joy is your natural state of being.

"Blessed are the Pure in heart for they shall see God."

Happy And Fortunate Are Those That Are Natural And Transparent – They See God In Everyone.

On the human level we observe the world of good and bad. But life is whole and there is a positive way to see it. That's what Jesus is talking about in this particular teaching.

"Judge not according to appearance but judge with a righteous judgment" ~John 7:24

Don't let the temporary appearance of something block what is real and true for you. Shakespeare said, "There is nothing either good or bad but thinking makes it so." The scripture also tells us to, think on the things that are pure, lovely, and true, of good report, beautiful and all that is contained in God's world. You cannot see God until you identify yourself as living in God's world.

Remember, nothing really happens TO you. Everything happens FOR you. Instead of seeing only in part, we want to see life from a holistic perspective. In the beginning of one's spiritual journey, it can be difficult to see God with physical eyes in the sense of locating the Divine in a particular place or time, or as a physical being you can walk up to and shake hands with, because God is Spirit.

The pure in heart are only looking to connect with the One Presence that shares only love, peace and acceptance. Jesus saw the good in all people and that was the secret of his healing power. You see the world, not as it appears outwardly, but as you are, and you are in spiritual unity with God. Purity of heart is not conflicted with many confusing thoughts. Once you release the attached thoughts which burden you, you will be free to see from a higher perspective, to see God in all things and in all beings.

"Blessed are the peacemakers: for they will be called children of God."

Happy And Fortunate Are The Creators Of Peace – They Are The Actualized Sons And Daughters Of God.

Why are the peacemakers so important? It is because they express the true nature of divinity in the highest sense. Peace is created inside of our beings through quiet contemplation. As we calm our minds and enter in to the realm of infinite, divine creativity, we develop a more peaceful state of being. There is a point of inner stillness at the center of your being. It is the meeting place of God and the human. Through the practice of allowing worrisome thoughts to become less and less, a calming spirit of peace grows more and more.

164

To be a peacemaker you first need to have peace. Violence begets violence and peace leads to more peace. Those with an agenda to control others through coercion in order to have peace do not really have peace. A creator of peace is able to reconcile the opposing forces and bring them together. It is not our job to make people become more peaceful. We are to facilitate peace through modeling it and setting an example. We have to make peace within ourselves first. In fact, when we do that we automatically become beings of a higher consciousness. The world is changed first and foremost by a change in our own consciousness. We teach it and live it ourselves. Whenever we take action from a positive consciousness, we make a difference. We cannot force change, but we can keep the idea alive in the face of those who put most of their energy into conflict.

It takes courage to speak your truth when the fashionable thing to do is poke fun at peacekeepers. Without peace-makers keeping the high watch, the world would literally descend into chaos. If everyone is only looking out for themselves and not each other, that would be one definition of "hell on earth."

Speak up and be bold! Believe in the ways of peace. Once you do, others will take notice and stand with you, not as bullies, but as peacekeepers for the highest benefit for all!

"Blessed are they that are persecuted for righteousness sake, for great is their reward in heaven."

Happy And Fortunate Are Those That Heal Their Inner Persecutor – They Will Live In A Happy Consciousness.

Certainly, being persecuted when you have done the right thing is one way to interpret this particular beatitude. However, there is a deeper meaning here.

Do you know anyone who has an inner persecutor? Do you have an inner tormentor? Whenever you align with the Divine, or start a new lifestyle and begin to exercise and eat healthy food your mind will often disagree with you and persecute you. "You really want that chocolate cake don't you?" "Just this one piece won't hurt will it?" "Do you really need to exercise today, after all, you are an important person that has a busy schedule to keep." "Let's just start the new program thing tomorrow, okay?"

Jesus was tested by his mind too. But he was able to rise above it because he understood how it works. It is our own "stinking thinking" that can get us into trouble very quickly. Temptations and persecutions always arise in the mind. Whenever you launch into a program of self-improvement through self-realization in order to change your thoughts, you will experience the slings and arrows of the inner persecutor. It is simply doing what it has been programmed by you to do. Press past the negativity and into the spirit of the mind on your spiritual journey to wholeness, where your Divine potential can be tapped.

Shift your attention away from problem thinking and focus on choosing new thoughts of self-empowerment. Practice thinking in the new way each day until it becomes second nature, your subconscious mind will accept the new belief and you will have established a new habit. Never give up and don't quit! Life wants to give you what you want but you must prove to yourself that you really want it by keeping the faith. Your mind can become a quiet sanctuary of calm and rest. Do not believe any negative thought that arises and you will get there!

That is where your reward lies...Inside of our own mind, where you will find the peace of God. Once you release the old mental patterns, peace arises, along with the spirit of joy, unconditional love and self-acceptance.

Now that's a heaven I can believe in!

Chapter Twenty

The Crucifixion

Jesus never said: *"God demands a sacrifice."*

"Your fear is 100% dependent on you for its survival."
~ Steve Maraboli

"The price of greatness is responsibility."
~ Winston Churchill

What does the crucifixion symbolize for us today? Did Jesus die for humanities sins because God was angry and desired a blood sacrifice to atone for our horrible sinful nature? What need would there be for blood being shed in order for someone to "pay" for our mistakes? What pleasure would God receive for having his Son killed? Was it a Divine idea to set up this bloody system of sacrifice? There are a lot of questions here, which need to be answered in order to understand what really went on in the Mind of God and the real reason Jesus died on the cross.

Here are some verses in the Bible not typically quoted or referred to:

"For I desire mercy, not sacrifice, and acknowledgment of God rather than burnt offering." ~ Hosea 6:6

"You do not delight in sacrifice, or I would bring it; you do not take pleasure in burnt offerings." ~ Psalm 51:16

"The multitude of your sacrifices-- what are they to me?" says the Lord. "I have more than enough of burnt offerings, of rams and the fat of fattened animals; I have no pleasure in the blood of bulls and lambs and goats." ~ Isaiah 1:11

"Sacrifice and offering you did not desire-- but my ears you have opened -- burnt offerings and sin offerings you did NOT require." ~ Psalm 40:6

The above verses answer the questions posed. The Mind of God does NOT delight in or take pleasure in blood sacrifices! Nor does God desire sacrifice and offerings! So if God did not send Jesus to die on the cross as a blood sacrifice for our sins, what was the real reason Jesus was crucified?

Inward Transformation

When Jesus came into the world. He came as a model or example of how a fully aware and awake human could live in harmony with all of life. This was something new to the Jewish people who, up until that time, required blood sacrifices for the moral failings of the people, whom they expected to commit errors and to break the law. Unless you were caught in the act, you got away with it and were not punished. It was strictly an outward law that never connected the heart with the behavior.

That is why Jesus said,

169

"Whoever thinks it in his mind has already done it."
~ Matthew 5:28

It is the inward transformation that becomes the cause for outward changes. It is your core beliefs, which create the experiences you have.

None of the characters in the Old Testament could live up to the demands of the law. Even David, who was said to be a "man after God's own heart", had one of his soldiers killed so he could take the man's wife for his own.

The world Jesus came into was a place of violence, war and bloody religious practices. Every day there were people lined up to bring an animal sacrifice to be slaughtered for their guilt and sins, as they were required to do by the law. If you told a lie and were caught, you would have to bring the animal to be sacrificed in the temple. The High Priest would lay his hands on you and transfer your sin and guilt to the animal, and then kill the animal in front of you. There was no magical power in this exchange. You merely satisfied the law and felt better because your sins were excused...until the next time.

In stark contrast to these two basic commandments of Jesus to "love God" and also to "love your neighbor", the Pharisees had created a complex system of 613 commandments, laws and rules. There were 365 negative commands and 248 positive laws. By the time Jesus arrived on the scene these laws had produced a cruel and arrogant system of do's and don'ts. The Priests were constantly adding new rules to further bind people to this harsh system that never really worked in the first place.

No Sacrifice, Only Love

However, the Mind of God in the Old Testament never wanted sacrifices. It was a system the priests used to make money from the people and to have power over them. (Hmmm...I wonder if that is what is happening today?) Do various religious leaders use the story of the cross to scare people and make them feel guilty?

Jesus allowed himself to be crucified on the cross to demonstrate *Agape*, which is Divine, Unconditional Love. *Agape* is expressed as the *realization of one's true value and worth*. It was not absolutely necessary for Jesus to die on the cross for our sins. The Mind of God does not even think in those terms! Jesus did it out of compassion for the people of that time. He saw their bloody religion and he desired for them to stop killing animals in a senseless way just to assuage their guilt. Therefore he said to them, "I will be a sacrifice for your guilt and fear."

Jesus understood that he was an eternal soul who would live forever...just as would the people he came to teach. He was willing to lay down his body to correct a flawed concept of God. He chose the path of Agape, which is the highest form of compassion. He understood the worth and value of humanity and was able to do this is because he was a fully mature Son of God. By comparison, most of the rest of the people were barely infants in their awareness of God, which is why they had such bloody practices. Jesus expressed his full potential as the Christ, and showed how love is willing to give on behalf of others.

He said,

"No greater love has a man than to lay down his life for his friends." ~ John 15:13

171

Some theologians say that Jesus had to die on the cross to satisfy the Divine sense of justice. The truth is that Jesus did it solely out of love and compassion for people, to help heal their state of mind and help them reconnect with their true innocence. Jesus was the mature Son of God. Jesus' strong desire to heal and forgive is his true message and his real mission.

The Apostle Paul

"Be transformed by the renewing of your mind."
~ Romans 12:2

Paul the Apostle had been a zealous Jew that knew the law forward and backward. So when he wrote his letters he was sharing from that viewpoint. Paul spent a lot of time trying to convince people of that time about the end of Jewish sacrifice and the need for transformational thinking. His self-identified purpose was to show the devout Jew how Jesus' death replaced the need for animal sacrifice and that forgiveness of each other through grace was the actual message of the gospel.

Paul himself spoke of a more advanced teaching.

*"Therefore leaving the elementary teaching about the Christ, let us press on to maturity, **not laying again** a foundation of repentance from dead works and of faith toward God."* *~ Hebrews 6:1*

He taught a simple message of healing their state of mind about sin and error thinking. There comes a point where forgiveness becomes a total surrender to God. In that "advanced" state, nothing is required and life is fully aligned with the inner Christ Presence.

172

Paul also suggested that the Gentiles, or non-Jews, were included in God's love. That was a hard truth for a "chosen people" to wrap their minds around. It must have been difficult for them to understand the words of Paul when he said,

> *"He is not a Jew which is one outwardly, but he is a Jew which is one inwardly and circumcision is that of the heart, in the spirit, not in the letter." ~ Romans 2:28*

This kind of truth had to be revealed from the inside and not everyone was able to accept it. There was so much confusion in the newly formed churches of that time. Some churches still continued to practice animal sacrifice, because it was so ingrained and was all they knew. Paul felt it was his mission to explain to them according to his understanding about what the crucifixion meant.

That is why renewing your mind is so important!

Jesus came to heal the perception of the people so they would no longer be under a law that didn't heal the heart or change the mind. They believed very deeply in their ability to make mistakes and lived at a fear filled level of conscious awareness. This was simply a part of the evolution of the collective soul's journey up to that point in history. Since **Jesus never said** humans were born into the world as sinners, there was no need for a blood sacrifice. Jesus was primarily out to change the perceptions, beliefs and attitudes of shame based thinking. Everything in life is really about how we think and perceive ourselves. If we believe we are bad then that is how we think, speak and act. If we understand that we are all children of God with real value and worth, then that will become our experience. Jesus, the healer of hearts and minds, wants you to believe in yourself and to grow into a mature son or daughter of God, and live your full Divine potential, just as he did.

All Means All

"In Adam all die but in Christ all are made alive."
~ I Corinthians 15:2

Notice the word *all* in that verse. *All* means *all* and not some! This is a gospel of inclusion rather than for just a few select groups. Adam represents the part of ourselves that is human, but the Christ is the Divine aspect, and is what truly saves, or heals us from our belief in sin and death. Spirit can never die, and spirit is what we are. It is only our false belief in sin consciousness that causes us to feel separate from God.

We are to stop believing so strongly in the shortcomings of human nature, and believe more fully in our Divine nature that has never actually been touched by this world. There is something inside all of us that wants to shine forth into the world. It is good and it is God within.

The crucifixion was not the real emphasis of the gospel, but rather, the teachings of love, life and truth. Those teachings are what align our hearts with the Christ consciousness within us all. Jesus simply did what Love would do in that situation.

Jesus said,

"Love one another as I have loved you."
~ John 13:34

The beauty of the cross is the revelation that love will do whatever it takes to express itself fully and completely. The

Creator has always only had loving thoughts about the creation, and from the beginning God said it was good!

What Jesus did was never about sacrifice - it was always about love. Let's focus on the life and teachings of Jesus the Christ and the example he set. Everything he did was about showing us the way to live an abundant and happy life. If you truly believe that he is the way of truth, peace and love then follow his example.

Immortality

"For this perishable must put on the imperishable, and this mortal must put on immortality. But when this perishable will have put on the imperishable, and this mortal will have put on immortality, then will come about the saying that is written, "Death is swallowed up in victory." ~ 1 Corinthians 15:53-54

Jesus demonstrated to us through his crucifixion that death is not what we think it is. Death is simply a transitional state, taking us from a physical experience to a spiritual expression of existence.

We all have a human egocentric way of living that has been created through the mistaken thinking of many generations. Sin is a metaphysical disease of the mind and is simply incorrect thinking, with actions that are not in harmony with our own divinity. Jesus showed us that dying, or releasing the old way of life, could raise us to new and higher states of being where the old rules no longer apply.
The metaphor of the caterpillar and the butterfly is a perfect analogy of what Jesus accomplished. The caterpillar has no clue about what life is like as a butterfly. These heavenly creatures do not have the same needs as the earthly creation. They are free to fly wherever they

want to go. They are now beyond the limitations of the previous existence. Unfortunately those who look at this saying from a literal perspective make Jesus' teachings more complicated than they need to be.

It's really about releasing the old patterns and embracing a higher way to live and expressing our true nature. The perishable or temporary human must put on the spiritual nature with its greater perspective of life. In the spiritual sense we never die or ever lose anything that is real. That which is real is eternal, and never fades or loses its essence.

The real you cannot die!

Did Jesus rise from the dead? Of course! He came forth from the tomb of limitation and proved that the soul never really dies. He was a spiritually mature Son of God who operated according to the rules of the higher nature that cannot die or be corrupted. Don't try to figure out the resurrected state from only a physical perspective or you will get bogged down like the caterpillar that is trying to figure out its true nature as a butterfly. When we understand the fact that Jesus overcame the "little mind", which is joined to the idea of separation, then we too can put away our mental and physical misperceptions and limitations and connect with our own higher nature. Our divine selves are waiting at the edge of our conscious awareness to connect with us.

"Therefore, if anyone is in Christ, he is a new creation. The old has passed away; behold, the new has come."
~ 2 Corinthians 5:17

If you are living and abiding in the Christ consciousness you are a totally new and different creation. The old habitual structures are passing and a new way of being is now appearing. *This is the complete healing of the separated mind that has been unaware of its true self.* Now will you accept who you are?

You are an eternal being who is one with God and all of life. Jesus did not really die in the sense of non-existence, but only changed forms to show us how we could do it too!

Little caterpillar, break free from your mental patterns and limited thinking and fully experience your transformation.

Dear butterfly, I will see you in the flower gardens of life... It is time to fly now!

Chapter Twenty-One

Intuition

Jesus never said: *"True worship is done primarily in beautiful and expensive temples made by religious institutions."*

"When the Spirit of truth comes, he will guide you into all the truth, for he will not speak on his own authority, but whatever he hears he will speak, and he will declare to you the things that are to come."
~ John 16:13

Cease trying to work everything out with your minds. It will get you nowhere. Live by intuition and inspiration and let your whole life be revelation."
~ Eileen Caddy

Spiritual truth also reveals itself to us through intuition. Intuition has been judged by some as having no value in a logical, rational world, because of our inability to measure it. Science has brought us many breakthroughs in medicine and technology over the last 100 years - the availability of indoor plumbing, computer technology, etc. The job of Science is to observe and objectively study that which needs examination, and gain understanding from an external viewpoint. Spiritual truth, on the other hand, lies hidden within us, and must be uncovered through direct experience on the inner level in order to fully understand it.

The early followers of Jesus were varied in their beliefs. They studied the teachings from a metaphorical perspective. Most considered them selves *Gnostics,* and they believed that spiritual truth could be perceived through enlightened revelation. They understood that truth came about from an *inner knowing or gnosis.*

It was not until around 355 AD that the Emperor Constantine determined which writings were acceptable and which were not. The Council of Nicaea burned many books, writings and letters so that their officially approved cannon could not be challenged. They chose books that supported their version of Jesus' teachings. Many *Gnostics* were considered heretics and were often killed because they disagreed with the power addicted Constantine. Fortunately, we can still get the truth from the canonized Bible when we approach it in an enlightened way.

Going Within

Have you ever wondered what it means to go within? Jesus is not saying that going within will lead us to physically finding God inside our liver or intestines. Rather, the idea of "intuit" can be broken down like this, *in-to-it.* If you want to have an intimate relationship with someone you must get inside him or her in a figurative way. To know what someone else knows you must get inside their head. If you want to understand how they feel about something you must get inside their heart.

When you really understand someone you will know and feel what they believe. It is impossible to really "get" someone unless you discover how to get inside him or her. We only allow people inside our hearts and minds if we have a trusting relationship with them. Without trust we are only working from the outside and are playing a guessing game. Deeper meaning is just that, we must go deep to uncover the true meaning that is there. Faith is trust in the positive and fear is trust in the negative. Either way you are trusting in something. Self-doubt is trust in those negative aspects of your self and believing more in your limitations than in your talent and ability to succeed. Trust is a decision to point your mind in a different direction. Trust is the surrender of the personality to the workings of the Higher Mind – to God.

The Sabbath

One of the many definitions of God is your breath and your very being. At anytime throughout the day, you can simply relax into your true nature and sense your connection with God. Relaxation helps you to unify and merge with the oneness that already exists within you. This is part of the teaching Jesus gave about the Sabbath and how to keep it holy. It was not just to take a day off from work each week as a religious observance. He was calling us into a relaxed and alert state of harmony with our Divine essence.

You are continually united with your purpose and destiny as you let go of your own expectations and allow the spirit within to guide you. This is the place of complete trust and total surrender. The holy Sabbath is a state of being that reflects perfect and utter trust in God and in your life. Everyday can become the Sabbath when you learn to rest in the awareness of the Presence of God.

"My words are spirit and they are life." ~ John 6:63

Jesus taught universal truths from the perspective of a spiritual mind. He spoke from the Divine point of view about issues that matter. Every one of us is a spiritual being first and foremost. We are having a human experience in every moment that sometimes veils our spiritual connection in such a way that it seems we are separate. The one spirit is the glue that holds all things together in a beautiful union and connects us all. We are the Divine body of God and we feed on the nourishing power of love. Love is a food required by all Souls that desire maturity and growth.

When Jesus spoke, his words were like a banquet of spiritual food and sustenance. Words infused with the spirit and energy of life are fulfilling and nourishing. They come from a place of wisdom, kindness and encouragement. These teachings are more than words to live by. They are our daily bread, which we need to live and stay spiritually connected to our Source. By feeding on the living word within our being we can learn to intuit our experiences and gain greater clarity and understanding.

Jesus never said the canonized Bible was the word of God!

Remember it is not the words on a page that give life. When we hear words of truth expressed from a spiritually minded person we gain understanding. Words spoken from an intuitive understanding bring life affirming energy to those who can hear it. The words come to life and create change and transformation in those with ears to hear.

"Faith comes by hearing the word of God."
~Romans 10:17

There is something about the spoken word that is able to relay powerful healing energies to its listeners. Often people find that they retain more information from audio books than from reading a book. But it goes deeper than that. It's the spirit within that teaches me the truth! No human can teach you the truth. They can only live it before you and inspire you to receive it. Truth arises from within. There is truth in the Bible for those who can interpret it spiritually and understand it from an inner state of divine awareness. Or, it can be a hammer that is used by the ego to beat people with, in order to make them submit. Forced submission takes away the choice of an individual and never really works. We are not meant to be mindless robots. Forcing people to obey what you think is right will ultimately create rebels who will run as far and as fast as they can to get away from that kind of control. An intuitive person does not have to manipulate another because they can feel and perceive the truth by going within.

Asking The Right Questions

It's important to question our beliefs from time to time in order to re-define what works and what does not. Life on earth is in constant flux, and that is the way it was made to be. If you don't allow for change you are resisting the natural flow. Everything changes and that is the law. The only option is to either resist the current or to go with the ongoing forward movement of the river of your life. By asking the right questions you can get answers that are helpful. *When the question feels right within, you can be sure the answer is on the way.* Guidance will fill your being when you ask the right questions.

The river of consciousness continues to move forward in a natural progression toward the beautiful flow of life, and it never stops. If it did, we would no longer exist. Eons ago many deserts on our planet were wonderful fertile places with an abundance of life and beauty. Now they are wastelands where life no longer flourishes. Without the proper conditions life cannot thrive.

Teach me your way, oh Lord, I will walk in your truth;
unite my heart to reverence your name (true nature).
Psalm 86:11

The inner Presence, or you might say, the Lord of your being knows how to bring the lessons into your life that gives you wisdom. To walk in the truth means that you choose to live in accordance with spiritual principles. This creates a sense of awe and wonder at the many signs and synchronicities that show up for you when you are walking in your truth. That means that when life seems to throw us a curve ball we stay true to our positive principles and trust that we are guided to where we need to be. Circumstance will continue to change and that is why we need the bedrock of truth to stand on. Life will unfold as it always does but I am centered within my own being. I am safe inside the haven of peace where God dwells, inside the holy temple of my body.

When you wish for things to remain the same you are standing still and not growing. From time to time it is necessary to reinvent yourself and go in a new direction. If not, you could become stuck in repetitious patterns from the past. Truth is always fresh and liberating. Many traditions can get stale over time and lose their power. Then new ideas are tried, new actions taken, and those, which satisfy by helping us grow closer to experiencing Truth, are adopted. Through this process, new ways of being are born. The essence of spiritual food is satisfying and does not insult your intelligence. Use your intuition to go within and uncover the wonders of your being.

Spirit can speak to us in many ways including dreams.

Guidance Through a Dream

For still the vision awaits its appointed time, it hastens to the end and it will not lie, if it seems slow, wait for it; it will surely come; it will not delay. Habakkuk 2:3

Several years ago our spiritual community was searching for a building with some land that would be able to accommodate our growing congregation. We had tried to close on three different properties but each time some kind of technicality held us up. We desired some acreage and water on the property too so we made our list of what we wanted and then we turned it over to the Higher Mind. Finally we let it go and decided to trust that what we needed would appear at the right time. One night after several months I had a dream. In the dream our Realtor took me to look at a property. The Realtor told me how much the property was and also where it was located. After we got there we pulled into the driveway and had to go through some fences. We drove around to the back of the property and there was some people standing there. Suddenly a petite woman stood up and looked at me with piercing eyes. I awoke with a start and proceeded to tell my wife about the dream. I instantly understood that a property would be showing up soon that would be what we were looking for. The petite woman represented a small window of opportunity to purchase the property and we would need to act quickly.

That next day I sat down at the computer and looked at an email from our Realtor. There it was, the property I had just dreamed about showing up on my computer screen. I immediately called our Realtor to find out about it. The location and the price were exactly what I had dreamed about! She called the owners and then called me back to let me know that the property had just come on the market and we had a short window of opportunity to see it and make a bid. We would have to go see it right away and make a fast decision on how much to offer.

We drove over to see the property that included 14 acres and a 3-acre lake. As we drove in through the fencing surrounding the property the hair on the back of my neck was standing at full attention. Everything matched what I had seen in the dream. We made an immediate offer and through some negotiation we bought the property. There were at least three other parties that made offers as well, but what made the difference was that Spirit had guided us all along!

This was divinely orchestrated for us and we are still enjoying the property today...

By listening to your intuition you can receive guidance that bypasses the logical mind. The higher mind knows about all of your options and which path is the best one to take. The idea is to learn to trust your inner guidance system to get what you need as you go along.

Jesus said,

I tell you the truth; the son can do nothing by himself. He does only what he sees the Father doing. Whatever the Father does, the son also does. ~John 5:19

In other words Jesus was following his guidance from within...

Chapter Twenty-Two

The Light of Enlightenment

Jesus never said: *"Sorry you weren't chosen, better luck next time..."*

"Then spoke Jesus again to them, saying, I am the light of the world: he that follows me shall not walk in darkness, but shall have the light of life." ~ John 8:12

We all know that light travels faster than sound. That's why certain people appear bright until you hear them speak." ~ Albert Einstein

The word light is found in the Bible 272 times and can be interchanged with the idea of enlightenment. Jesus was totally focused on bringing enlightenment to the world. His whole mission was to introduce spiritual principles, which would bring the light of awareness and a deeper understanding to people.

The teaching of enlightenment is not always easy to get across because of the lack of self worth many people experience. It was easier for the clergy to turn these spiritual ideas into rules that make people good and bad rather than whole and well.

The Single Eye

In the New Testament the Greek word for *world* is *kosmos* and means *the ordered arrangement of the current world system*. Jesus knew the current *kosmos* at the time needed to be changed, and the way to do that was through Divine ideas. If people could repent *or change their mind*, they could begin to experience a different arrangement of beliefs, which would result in a higher quality of life.

It's time for humanity to grow up and put away our childish behavior, not through coercion or force, but through the inner process of enlightenment.

"If your eye be single then your whole body will be filled with light." ~ Luke 11:34

The eye is the concentrated focus of the mind, the razor sharp intention and attention that cuts through the unnecessary and reveals what is real and true. Commonly referred to as our third eye, it is spiritual in nature and helps us see into what is really valuable and important. We can all access it by using, developing and refining our ability to focus on truth. Jesus is saying that when you gain this single focus within your inner body of consciousness, your genuine self would be illuminated and you will discover your true spiritual purpose. Enlightenment is revealed within you when this eye of perception is opened and understanding begins to flood your being.

In Service to the Light

"Let your light so shine before men, that they may see your good works, and glorify your Father which is in heaven." ~ Matthew 5:16

The goal of enlightenment is to shed the old ways of being, thinking and perceiving so that we can live from an inner state of knowing and divine awareness. If you want an enlightened life, then you will need to find the light that Jesus was speaking about.

The light within us is the Christ consciousness that is beyond the attachments to the physical form. The more enlightened you become, the more you will see that the reason for life is actually to serve others. We are all inter-connected by the One Spirit. We are here to use what we have been given to support the whole. We are not doing these good works for any reason other than it is ours to do and brings us joy in the process.

Many people today are suffering, doing work they do not love or enjoy. It is a major cause of unhappiness. The material world can sometimes blind us to our true inner glory. When we fix our gaze upon this outer world of effects, our inner light seems to dim. If the only thing you feed upon is fear and negativity, then that is what you will continue to create. We must mature to the point where we are not overcome or overwhelmed by how things appear outwardly.

Jesus said,

"Do not judge according to external appearance, but judge with proper judgment." ~ John 7:24

Proper judgment means making a decision in alignment with the truth by determining what is real and what is not. Instead of the word *proper* some versions of the Bible use the word *righteousness,* which is the view from the Divine perspective.

As we become more enlightened we tend to look at everything from that Divine perspective. We look for the higher purpose in every event that happens and in every person we see. As we do, the outer world starts to line up with the way we see it. But first we have to see it "right" for it to show up that way. This is the single focus we need. It is not a denial of what is already appearing, but it is the out-picturing of reality from the God Mind within that makes all things new.

This kind of visioning comes through us by revelation within the inner self. In order for the world to reflect its perfection outwardly in our lives, we need to envision the perfection as it really is inwardly, and bring it forth. Even the mind's perceived imperfection is really perfect at whatever stage we happen to be. Once we stop using the analytical mind as our main mode of perception, and stop judging according to outward appearance, we can live a more enlightened life.

"Walk in the light as he is in the light." ~ 1ˢᵗ John 1:7

Darkness is the absence of light rather than its opposite. We all can only walk in the light that we have. On the human level it looks as if we are seeking the light and allowing it to become integrated into life. On the other side of the veil, consisting of mental beliefs and limitations, the Divine is calling us to the light. We are being pulled to this higher awareness of a greater state of being and it is Divinity that is drawing us. Even though it feels like you are doing it all yourself, you are actually being guided by a higher Intelligence.

Mystery

"Behold, I show you a mystery: We shall not all sleep; but we shall all be changed in a moment, in the twinkling of an eye, at the last trumpet. For the trumpet shall sound, and the dead shall be raised incorruptible, and we shall be changed. For this corruptible must put on incorruption, and this mortal must put on immortality."
~1st Corinthians 15:51-53

Metaphysically, the above verse could be interpreted as:

I now reveal to you a sacred secret that you are being brought into. We will not all remain in a state of unconsciousness. You are being changed in the smallest molecules of your being, through the revealing of a single-minded focus, and through the full experience of the final message you are now ready to hear. By completely absorbing this higher teaching, your consciousness will be raised to a state where you no longer accept your limitations as valid, and you will be transformed in the process. As you release your beliefs of lack and limitation, then your lower nature will transform like the butterfly, no longer an earthly caterpillar, but a completely brand new creation that has never before existed.

It's time to receive the "last trumpet," or the complete message of enlightenment, so we not only liberate ourselves but the rest of creation as well.

Chapter Twenty-Three

Caught Up

Jesus never said, *"All the good folk will fly off the earth and go "over yonder" to a planet called heaven."*

"I know a man in Christ who fourteen years ago was caught up to the third heaven. Whether it was in the body or out of the body I do not know--God knows."
~II Corinthians 12:2

"After that, we who are still alive and are left will be caught up together with them in the clouds to meet the Lord in the air. And so we will be with the Lord forever."
~1st Thessalonians 4:17

As a young teenager I was taught the idea of a secret rapture that was to come and take us off the earth and bring us into heaven, somewhere "out there." This idea represents the ultimate in escapism from our responsibilities, and that is not the point of life. We are here to master ourselves and bring heaven to earth...not escape the world.

Several places in the New Testament speak of being caught up and these scriptures are best interpreted symbolically. Paul was *caught up* and had a *spiritual experience* that was hard for him to talk about. He wasn't sure if he was in or out of the body at the time. Obviously this experience had a profound effect on Paul and his life. He never left the planet to gain this wisdom. It all happened within him. 1st Thessalonians 4:17 quoted above is also Paul's writing. He was speaking of the same experience here too, that spiritual enlightenment is actually for anyone who wants it. We can all have our own rapturous and enlightening experience with God. Once you reach a certain quality of refined awareness, you automatically become a candidate for this experience.

Music of the Spheres

To be "caught up in the air" is the idea of merging with the invisible world of spirit as *air represents a higher element* than the physical dimension of earth. We are the earthly caterpillars destined to become a creature of the *air* called a butterfly. We move out of the heavier density to exist in a lesser density where the physical adapts to a greater spaciousness and a lighter frequency. The music of the spheres plays all around us but we cannot hear the sounds with our physical ears. But we can learn to tune in to the higher frequencies of sound and light.

Several years ago I was making a daily trip to work that took about one half hour to make. During this time I practiced being empty of thought and focused on my conscious awareness. One day as I was driving the freeway I began to hear some beautiful music that seemed to be coming from everywhere. I checked the radio and it was off, then I rolled down the window but it was not coming from outside the car either. That is when I realized that it was arising from somewhere inside my being. It was definitely beyond the earth and was "in the air" so to speak.

Another experience I had as a sophomore in high school was similar. As a young teen I suffered the ups and downs of teenage angst. I was experiencing some depression and needed some help and encouragement. One day, while sitting in an economics class I was feeling so low that I was close to tears, when suddenly I heard music that seemed to be coming from another room. At first I thought it was the choir rehearsing and singing. It was very loud but no one in the room seemed to be hearing it. That is when one of the voices began ascending octaves that I had never heard before or since. It was beyond human capabilities and as the voice went higher my spirits rose upward with the melody. I was changed completely in that moment in a way I will never forget. I was totally lifted out of my depression into a state of joy and rapture.

Over the years I have come across many people who have had similar experiences, leading me to believe that there is more going on *"in the air"* than we have yet to imagine!

People are Clouds

Another aspect of this verse is the understanding of what *clouds* are. Clouds can be people or beings that exist at a higher rate of vibration.

"Therefore, since we are surrounded by such a great cloud of witnesses." ~ *Hebrews 12:1*

From this verse we see the metaphorical perspective of clouds as being witnesses to our growth. They are cheering us on, even assisting us in our process of growth and enlightenment. These clouds are "in the air," often whispering to us through faint feelings or intuition, that we are on the right track. They give us a nudge here or there. In moments of clarity, we get caught up and meet these glorious clouds "in the air" gaining insight into our lives.

193

The last part of the verse says, "so shall we be with the Lord forever." Every person has access to that master consciousness state when they are open to it. This self-mastery is on a level such that we can never go back to the misunderstandings of the past. Once you ascend in consciousness you are going from glory to glory, to ever evolving heights, and discovering greater states of bliss and joy.

It's not about escaping your trials and being lifted off the planet. Spiritual maturity is about facing your deepest fears and uncovering their falsehood, and unveiling the truth of the glory that resides within. Begin where you are on your path right now. Search your own being and you will find the Christ Presence that has been waiting patiently for you. There is nowhere to go geographically because YOU are the habitation of God, right here, right now.

Welcome to God's world...you are the Kingdom of Heaven and you are God's world!

Chapter Twenty-Four

Mystical Christ

Jesus Never said: *"God is divided into three distinct personalities that make up a trinity."*

"One Lord, one faith, one baptism, one God and Father of all, who is over all and through all and in all."
~ Ephesians 4:5-6

"For in one Spirit we were all baptized into one body— Jews or Greeks, slaves or free—and all were made to drink of one Spirit." ~ 1ˢᵗ Corinthians 12:13

Life takes on a deeper dimension when you are immersed in the spirit of love and oneness. Have you ever felt there was more going on than what the physical eyes could see, and that life was a mystery to be explored and enjoyed?

As a child I felt connected to everyone and everything. I lived in the ocean of spiritual consciousness, until I got older and people begin to teach me separation (and I bought it!). What is called Holy Spirit is the Universal Presence in which we all live. Just as all the fish are contained within the dimension of the ocean, we are all swimming in a sea of spirit. We are all energy beings connected by the One Spirit in a beautiful oneness of spiritual life, whether we are in the body or beyond. While

195

some may claim that God is three distinct personalities, God is both One and The Many. The number three is simply the idea of completion. We are all a part of the Godhead, and all of us have our own divinity to explore. We have been taught such a watered down version of Jesus' teachings that it's difficult for many people to believe they are Divine - but we are.

This is the real mystery of life: We are more than physical beings. We are eternal souls that live on forever. We are the image of God, but we "see into the glass darkly" and do not recognize our own image. Jesus came to remind us of our glory and oneness with the Father. Jesus is a mirror in which we can see our own reflection.

"What's in a name? That which we call a rose by any other name would smell as sweet..." ~ Shakespeare

It is the lack of this awareness that makes people afraid. As you grow in spiritual consciousness you begin to lose concern over all differences. Instead, you start to appreciate all the variety and diversity of life. Everyone has a little different pigmentation of skin color. Just as you can enjoy the various colors of red, yellow or white roses, neither is intrinsically better than another, they are simply different. It is the same with human beings. We have just enough differences to make it interesting. It would be ludicrous to judge one color of rose as bad and another as good. They are all unique roses with their own glory and beauty...and they all smell good!

We are all part of the one race, the human race. We are family, and as family, we can take care of each other if we choose too. If we don't choose to, a part of us suffers.

We are both human and divine. We currently live in a physical world but it is only temporary. Spirit cannot die but it can change forms. God can appear in any way, shape or form that she pleases. And she does.

All of us contain the same Christ Spirit that dwelled in Jesus. Just because we have not fully realized who we are does not make us any less than Jesus. God is appearing as the individualized expression of you right now.

The entire universe was made for you as a school of learning and development. It is quite something to ponder the vastness of space into which we may grow. We are these ever-evolving beings with huge potential just waiting to be tapped and released.

Jesus, as well as other great spiritual teachers, broke through and paved the way. We can now follow that way and become what we were always meant to be.

"Truly, truly, I say to you, he who believes in Me, the works that I do, he will do also; and greater works than these he will do; because I go to the Father." ~ John 14:12

I do not understand it all, but the one thing I know for sure is, "You haven't seen anything yet." We are just beginning to catch a glimmer of who we are. Once our eyes adjust to the brightness of the light within, we will catch a ride on the wave of glory and ascend to a higher level of spiritual evolution. You are a deep mystery and there is so much more to discover. We have seen enlightened beings that have made a difference whenever a difference needed to be made. Enlightened ones such as Mahatma Gandhi and Martin Luther King changed the world forever through their teaching of non-violence. There have been inventors, physicists, schoolteachers, scientists, philosophers, and many more who came from all walks of life, who inwardly knew there was something beyond their current limitations. We are catching a vision of the mystical Christ who already knows the way home. You will get there all in your own timing and on your own path.

Wondering...

To be a mystic is to live in a state of awe and wonder. It means you know that life is a mystery and so are you. Therefore, you approach life with a beginner's mind and with an open heart. You constantly use your creative imagination to wonder about the many mysteries your life holds. This approach is perfect for reflection and contemplation.

You must become as a little child to enter the kingdom state of being.

One of the amazing attributes of children is their ability to wonder about everything and to be curious. The innocence of a child allows them to ask the questions adults stopped asking long ago. Children love using their imagination and the whole world is their playground.

This wondering state is the beginning of realization.

Wondering: *"To desire and be curious about something, ponder, think about, meditate on, reflect on, muse on, puzzle over, speculate about, marvel, be amazed and be astonished, to stand in awe." ~ Webster's Dictionary*

How old were you when you were told to stop dreaming and to be realistic? It usually happens pretty early in childhood. We call it socialization. You go to school and teachers often focus on the left half of the brain, not realizing that education needs to be a whole brain approach. We need to develop both the right and the left side of the brain to be balanced. The state of wondering and the feeling of awe are what open us up to the mysteries of life. When you take time to ponder about something and meditate on it, you will receive answers. It's not always about answering the left-brain's questions; sometimes it's the inner feeling of peace and contentment you really need. A truthful answer always feels good, always brings you peace, and always sets you free.

Wondering is the receptive state necessary before one can enter in to higher consciousness. The Psalmist David said,

"I will enter his gates with thanksgiving in my heart."
~Psalm 100:4

What are you most grateful and thankful for?

Ponder it every day and see where that takes you. Once you start to give thanks and praise for your life, Spirit begins to talk to you. The Christ Spirit will woo you and bring you in to a state of spiritual Presence that is awesome or *full of awe*!

You will discover more things to be in *awe* about. You will even find yourself in *awe* of the microcosm or the so-called insignificant stuff of life.

My wife and I have birdfeeders outside our office window at home and we are constantly watching a variety of birds fly in and out. I marvel at the way they can descend from a tree branch or the way they come and go taking turns feeding. We even love it when the squirrel hangs upside down on the birdfeeder trying to get food. It is the play of the Divine in our back yard! God is amusing herself with it all. We are "a mused" too! Nature becomes our *muse* to discover the Infinite Intelligence hidden in plain sight.

Entering In...

As I look at Creation I begin to get a glimpse of the character and nature of divinity.

God likes to smile and to laugh!

The top videos on YouTube are pet videos. Why? Because cats and dogs are hysterical – that's why! They are so darned cute!   In their play they are curious about everything. God is showing up as your cat or dog to teach you how to play and how to reconnect with higher unconditional love and joy. There is a blissful joy beyond words you can experience for yourself. Dogs are so caught up in the ecstasy of moment-to-moment awareness that they constantly wag their tails in absolute joy. Do you know why they bark and howl? Because they can!

They don't need a reason. It just feels right to bark at the postal worker. When one dog howls they all tend to start howling. If you are a dog it is the thing to do and it feels so good!

Once you stop waiting around for reasons to be happy and start wondering and musing about everything with a playful curiosity you might start howling too! Let your self go a little and get excited about life as it is right now. Look at what's around you and ponder it awhile. For instance, look at your hands and then feel the energy that flows through them. If you don't feel anything then ponder them until you do. If you have a pulse it means you are alive and that means energy is moving through you like a river.

Once you spend some time wondering, then you can enter into "the more abundant life" Jesus talked about. You finally get the cosmic joke and it is truly hilarious. Have you ever watched the Dalai Lama being interviewed? He is constantly laughing as if he has the inside scoop on what life is about. In fact all the insiders or those that have "entered into" know something that most people don't know.

It's all really very simple...Life is amazing and that is the point of it!

Once you enter into the fully aware Presence of life its beauty will astound you. Most people have not really seen the inner glory of life's true essence. One person looks at a waterfall and says, "That's nice." Another person catches their breath and experiences the wonder and power of the moment. They see a rainbow reflected in the water and swear it is the most beautiful waterfall they have ever seen. They have entered into another state of being, another state of consciousness, another state of awareness where everything they see is as if it were for the first time, with the wonder and open heart of a child.

It may be hard for some people to grasp and really understand that there is a mystical aspect of life. There is a glory hidden in everything and everyone, including you! You can intensify this experience of wonder and amazement by being fully conscious of seeing, listening and touching. Your senses are heightened and even the breath is delicious and sensual. The present moment deepens and you are in love with all of life.

Realization

Do you remember watching The Wizard of Oz as a child? In the beginning, everything was black and white with no colors. It was a little grainy looking and it all appeared very dull. Then...when Dorothy was *"caught up"* into the Land of Oz, the colors came into view and it was spectacular. Everything vibrated and there were strange beings flying about. There was so much color that the kids watching it would "...oooh" and "...aahh." The stark contrast greatly intensified the depth of color and the richness of the scenery.

When we begin to notice the true elegant beauty in it all, we are waking up to God's world. This is what realization is and it has been there all the time. We just did not see it. See the deep mystery unfold and allow it to upload into your being. Using words to describe a sacred experience is nearly impossible. Poetic language is the best way to describe realization. That is why the Bible is not literal because then it is just black and white, with no color or imagination, and it becomes a dead letter.

Quiet Beauty

True beauty arises from within the silence. Trees do not speak, yet they teach us much. Sunshine doesn't say anything verbally, but it shines it's light on us all. Everything we see arises from silence. I look out my window and there are six new goslings walking around on our property. They were not there just a few days ago. Life is arising and taking on various shapes and forms and then changes again. My physical form is different than it was a few years ago and my inner self has changed too. All of it arises from the quiet beauty of Divine Grace.

I invite you to experience the mystic Christ that abides within you. Your realization will be personal and it may be difficult to explain to others, because it is truly indescribable.

All of us have it but not all of us are aware...yet.

We are talking about a greater sense of aliveness, a larger awareness of your life's purpose that brings you joy and leads to a deeper experience of love in all of your relationships. We are moving from being unconscious to becoming more conscious of what is already available to us in the here and now.

Jesus told us, *"Rivers of living water will flow from within them." ~John 7:38*

There is a well inside you and once you tap into it, *"you will never thirst again." ~John 14:14*

Chapter Twenty-Five

The Gospel of Healing and Forgiveness

Jesus Never Said: *"I have some really "bad news" for you...most of you will be tortured forever in hellfire!"*

"This is the time of fulfillment. The kingdom of God is at hand. Repent, and believe in the gospel." ~ Mark 1:15

The word gospel literally means good news. Jesus came proclaiming the good news of the inner Kingdom that everyone could access and enjoy. He was not speaking about an outward kingdom that he would rule over someday. He spoke of a spiritual kingdom that is found within the heart and mind of every person. The kingdom was near and at hand and all you had to do was repent, which means to change your mind, and believe in the good news rather than the bad news the priests were sharing at the time. Ego driven religious beliefs are constantly focused on sin, lack, fear and dread. These beliefs do not lead to life but rather to sickness, stress, trouble and pain. Jesus was a healer and shared tools to help facilitate forgiveness and healing for all.

"For this people's heart has grown dull and with their ears they can barely hear, and their eyes they have closed, lest they should see with their eyes and hear with their

*ears and understand with their heart and turn, and I
would heal them." ~Mark 13:15*

This scripture gets to the heart of the matter - and to a deeper problem. The spiritual heart has become dull and has lost the sensitivity to the refined energies of love and joy. People have lost the sense of the presence of God in their own being. This lack of spiritual awareness keeps them deaf and blind to what is really important. Jesus used his teachings to awaken hearts to another reality beyond the physical world of materiality. If you have ever been in relationship with someone that is hard of hearing, it can prove to be frustrating for both parties. It can be difficult to communicate effectively when one cannot understand the other and it can often lead to misunderstanding. A heart that is covered over with the fears and concerns of this world will make it difficult for them to enjoy their divine connection. Jesus' message was given to heal a spiritual problem. This beautiful poetic language from the Bible reveals quite a bit about what Jesus was doing in his ministry.

Spiritual Therapy

The word for "heal" in the Greek is *therapeuo* – it's where we get our word for therapy. Jesus was applying a spiritual therapy to heal the hearts of people. Most people think Jesus was healing the physical body and that is why they were following him. The truth is that Jesus was working directly with the core issues of disease. He didn't come to heal only the outward; it was the heart Jesus was after! The heart is where true healing happens. What is the heart? The heart is your true essence and it's where your true spiritual identity is contained. It is the part of you that looks and searches for fulfillment and meaning. For many people, it just feels like an aching hole and they try to find anything to plug the hole and relieve the pain.

Feelings of emptiness, loneliness and insecurity are signs of an unfulfilled life. The cause is a loss of connection to a spiritual union with divinity. We were born to be the habitation of Divine Spirit, and that is our true calling. We are the house of God and nothing else can fill that space.
Jesus' real mission was to bring healing therapy to people. From him, we learn the power of healing words as the people felt his gentle touch and were awakened. We are energetic beings and Jesus was a master at working with energy to help them receive what they needed. By observing Jesus and learning his ways of using healing energy, the disciples were able to do the same work. When you are out of alignment with your heart energy, you can become stuck. Because this stuck energy has nowhere to go, it can cause illness and disease to show up in your body.

Forgiving The Unforgivable

"I say to you, all sins and all blasphemies that people utter will be forgiven them. But whoever blasphemes against the Holy Spirit will never have forgiveness, but is guilty of an everlasting sin." ~ Mark 3:28-30

The blasphemy "that is unforgivable" is of the person who dishonors themselves or others and refuses to practice forgiveness. We are the habitation of God and Holy Spirit lives in all of us. Therefore when we hold others and ourselves in anger, hatred or bitterness we become stuck. As long as we remain in this state, we push away our good and our healing. In the Lord's Prayer, Jesus said, "We cannot be forgiven until we forgive." Forgiveness is letting go and through repentance (changing the mind) and self-release, we are healed and forgiven. There is nothing that is unforgivable - unless you refuse to forgive yourself! You must apply the true healing therapy of Divine love and self-care and learn to be gentle with yourself.

You are a child of God and you don't deserve to be criticized and condemned, by others and certainly not by your own mind. Healing comes when you allow yourself time to relax and bathe in loving self-acceptance. Treat yourself the way you really want to be treated. You are not a mistake. You are only "in error" when you punish yourself for your missteps. God loves you perfectly and unconditionally – just as you are. If you really want to show your gratitude, do it by showering yourself with love. Once you are healed, you become a witness to the awesome power of forgiveness and love. There is nothing that is unforgivable. Everything is washed away in the waters of self-compassion and complete acceptance.

Everyone has a common need to forgive and be forgiven. Our world is, in many ways, hostage to old resentments and many thousands of year's worth of ancient hostilities. Wars have been going on for so long that sometimes we can't remember why. People hold grudges their ancestors originally held, because that is what they learned to do! Healing the world is simple...we must forgive and we must be forgiven. If you focus your energy on the healing power of forgiveness you become a catalyst for world change.

The End Of The Age Of Suffering

"And this gospel of the kingdom will be preached in the whole world as a testimony to all nations, and then the end will come." ~ Matthew 24:14

Once everyone is aware of the good news of healing and forgiveness, we can experience the end of the old age of fear, judgment and resentment. The gospel is the message of forgiveness. God is NOT mad at you. You are a child of God and you can heal yourself by letting go of the past. You need to take the first step and begin to practice the true healing art of forgiveness.

Our world needs role models to demonstrate how to live free from attachments to anger and bitterness. We need some heroes that can divest themselves of their ancient fears and fully live as mature sons and daughters of God.

I have read many articles and blogs by some authors that try to prove that people are different today than they use to be. However, what was true then is still true now - everyone has similar needs; to give and receive love; to have a peaceful family and community where we are accepted as we are, and to be inspired and guided in our lives.

Mature spiritual leadership is on the rise and we need powerful healers who know how to move energy and how to create change. Who are these people that I am referring to? People like you and me, who have faced our shadow side and are now free to talk about it.

You don't have to be perfect to be a healing force in the world. You simply need to own your connection with divinity and desire to ignite that connection in others.

Sacred Love

We are one with God. What does oneness feel like? It feels like Sacred Love.

We experience healing by having an inward revelation of sacred love. One way this revelation can come is through the kindness and care of others. The energy of Sacred Love can also be channeled through us and become a healing influence for the people we focus upon. By putting positively focused attention on the people around us, we share our love with them. Unconsciousness is the opposite of love. If you are not taking the time to notice the people in your daily life, you are missing the point of your existence. It is attention and awareness that creates the atmosphere for the expansion of love.

There are some who are sleepwalking through life, shuffling down the road trying to get to the next thing they have to do. Everyone is in a hurry and red lights are ignored more than ever before because of the need to get someplace else, and fast. But it's not just because they are in a hurry, it's because they don't want to be where they are - a place that feels empty and incomplete. The hope is that the next stop, the next relationship or the next job will finally make them happy. Sadly, it never does. The emptiness continues until attention is given to what is going on in their lives now, in this moment.

We need spiritual therapy that gets to the heart of our real needs. You can be a spiritual healer by coming from a holistic place within. We need those who speak the gentle words of comfort; care and healing to others need to hear it. Abusive religious beliefs and the image of a fearful, angry God ready to punish us have caused many people to harden or shut down. They need to be opened and gently guided to a safe place within and they need patience, kindness, and a listening ear. A Spiritual Healer is a generous spirit that will model the abundant life that is available to all. Once you can express your divinity outwardly toward others, healing will happen everywhere you are.

You can help redefine and heal the misunderstandings many have about divinity. Jesus shared an intimate connection with Divinity, which is in the midst of us, and not far off in space. Someone once said, "There is no spot where God is not." The Spirit of Life is found within the drug addict and any other hurting person too. In the midst of confusion is where Sacred Love can be found. You access it by changing your mind and looking at the "last place on earth" most people would expect to find divinity. Right here. Right where you are, God is.

"Then Jesus approached and said to them, "All power in heaven and on earth has been given to me. Go, therefore, and make disciples of all nations, baptizing them in the name of the Father, and of the Son, and of the Holy Spirit, teaching them to observe all that I have commanded you. And behold, I am with you always, until the end of the age." ~ Matthew 28:18-20

Here is my interpretation of this verse of scripture.

I have achieved self-mastery of my spiritual and physical dimensions. Now it is your turn to do the same. Go, and bring enlightenment to all and they will follow you into the spiritual oneness I have demonstrated through my relationship to the Father within, and through the union and emersion of Holy Spirit. Teach the universal principles that I shared with you and I will be with you in spirit until the end of all your suffering!

When you read the gospels from a positive and intuitive perspective the teachings of Jesus will reveal to you a state of grace and wonder that will transform your life. Divine Love will enfold you and keep you safe until the end of all of your suffering. Nothing will be impossible to you!

"Truly I say to you, whoever says to this mountain, 'Be taken up and cast into the sea,' and does not doubt in his heart, but believes that what he says is going to happen, it will be granted." ~Mark 11:23

Through the motivation of love and the power of our faith, we can move some mountains together and share some really Good News!

Peace

76434246R00119

Made in the USA
Columbia, SC
09 September 2017